BLACK
TRAILBLAZERS

BLACK TRAILBLAZERS

30 COURAGEOUS VISIONARIES WHO BROKE BOUNDARIES, MADE A DIFFERENCE, AND PAVED THE WAY

BIJAN BAYNE   ILLUSTRATED BY JOELLE AVELINO

Andrews McMeel
PUBLISHING®

Andrews McMeel Publishing
a division of Andrews McMeel Universal
1130 Walnut Street, Kansas City, Missouri 64106

www.andrewsmcmeel.com

22 23 24 25 26 POA 10 9 8 7 6 5 4 3 2 1

ISBN: 978-1-5248-7477-3

Library of Congress Control Number: 2022930758

Editor: Allison Adler
Art Director: Katie Jennings Campbell
Production Editor: Elizabeth A. Garcia
Production Manager: Julie Skalla

Made by:
Asia Pacific Offset
Address and location of production:
Building 10 No. 2, Qimeng Smart Park, West Lake Industrial Zone,
Xikeng Community, Yuanshan Street,
Longgang District, Shenzhen 518115, China
1st Printing — June 13, 2022

ATTENTION: SCHOOLS AND BUSINESSES
Andrews McMeel books are available at quantity discounts with bulk
purchase for educational, business, or sales promotional use.
For information, please e-mail the Andrews McMeel Publishing
Special Sales Department: specialsales@amuniversal.com.

CONTENTS

INTRODUCTION

THINK OF THE WORLD AS YOU KNOW IT TODAY, where astronauts travel to outer space, where science and medicine save and enrich lives, where culture is bold and vibrant, where technology is at your fingertips, and where regular citizens can become powerful voices for good. All this would not be possible without the unrelenting efforts of Black trailblazers throughout history.

A *trailblazer* is a person who comes to a rough patch in the forest with no obvious route forward, and instead of turning back around, they come up with a new idea, they rally others for help, or they devise a plan for how to create a new path forward. They blaze their own trail, which allows others to follow behind them. And when someone becomes a trailblazer, it can be in just about anything—from science and medicine, to freedom from injustice, to books and music, to confidence in oneself.

Take mathematician Katherine Johnson (page 53), who didn't use a computer to calculate the path to the moon. She *was* the computer—and for many decades, she wasn't even a footnote in the history books. Imagine doing a good deed and giving blood for someone who might need it in an emergency. Our ability to save that blood to give it to someone else is all thanks to Charles Drew (page 37). Or think of how you can move about freely—on a bus, at a voting booth, or at a water fountain—without a rule that says you don't belong because of the color of your skin. Without civil rights activists like Claudette Colvin (page 93), Diane Nash (page 89), and Martin Luther King, Jr. (page 69), among many others, those freedoms might not be possible.

Changemakers throughout history take on many different forms, and it's not always obvious who those people are. Even if someone doesn't call themselves an activist, that doesn't mean they aren't making a difference. The actions of those who came first allow other people to continue the work of progress. Quincy Jones (page 85) paved the way for Black musicians, filmmakers, and producers. Florence Griffith Joyner (page 113) and Misty Copeland (page 125) showed young women that the sky is the limit no matter what they look like. And Barack Obama (page 117) and Kamala Harris (page 121) made it clear that Black and Brown boys and girls can grow up to lead the world.

Some of these names are familiar, but so many of these important innovators have been written out of the story, when they *are* the story. Read on about these 30 *Black Trailblazers,* the inspiring pioneers whose indispensable work propelled the world forward and set the course of history.

PHILLIS WHEATLEY

WRITER AND POET   BORN: 1753 · DIED: 1784

- **First published Black woman in the American colonies**
- **Personally invited to meet future president George Washington**

The woman we know as Phillis Wheatley was born with another name in West Africa, where a local chief sold her into slavery when she was just 7 or 8 years old. A slave trader then brought her to the American colonies in a ship with hundreds of other people he planned to sell. When she arrived in Boston on July 11, 1761, a wealthy man named John Wheatley bought the frightened young girl to work for his wife. They called her Phillis after the name of the slave ship that brought her to the colonies and Wheatley for the family she was forced to serve.

The Wheatley family took a special interest in Phillis's education. Quickly recognizing her talents for language, they even assigned her housework to their other enslaved people so that she could focus on her studies. In many places, teaching an enslaved person to read was illegal. Phillis not only read, but she read Mr. Wheatley's own collection of famous writers. By the age of 12, she could read complex works in English, Greek, and Latin. Phillis especially loved to read classic poets like Homer and John Milton, whose works inspired her to write.

"SINCE MY RETURN TO AMERICA MY MASTER, HAS AT THE DESIRE OF MY FRIENDS IN ENGLAND GIVEN ME MY FREEDOM." —PHILLIS WHEATLEY

She published her first poem in a local paper when she was just 14 years old. By the time she turned 18, Phillis had 28 poems she hoped to print as a collection. The Wheatleys, who had been happy to show off their talented ward to friends and family, did their best to find a publisher. When no one in the colonies would consider the work of an enslaved person, they turned to their connections in England.

In 1773, Phillis accompanied Nathaniel Wheatley to London, where her work was already being celebrated. People were curious about the enslaved African girl who could write and recite so well. During her trip, she read for the mayor and secured the support of a wealthy countess, who helped Phillis publish her book that same year. Upon her return to Boston, the Wheatleys offered her something she longed for even more than publication. After 13 years of being owned by other people, Phillis was finally free.

Having her freedom didn't mean having it easy, though. Phillis still had to prove herself to people who didn't believe a Black girl who had been enslaved could have written so beautifully. At one point, a group of Boston politicians and doctors took it upon themselves to "examine" Phillis to see if she was legit.

THE WRITE STUFF

Phillis often used her talents to write letters to famous men expressing her opinions and support. She wrote one of these powerful letters to Revolutionary War general (and future U.S. president) George Washington. The general, who was busy commanding all the colonial troops against the British, invited the author to meet him. In March of 1776, Phillis met General Washington in Cambridge, Massachusetts. Four months later, he led the colonies to win their independence from England.

A LONG HISTORY

Famous French philosopher Voltaire once said Phillis was proof a Black person could write poetry. Considering that Homer and Aesop—two of the most well-known poets of all time—were likely Black, this is pretty ridiculous. In fact, Black people had been writing poems in Ethiopia, Egypt, and Spain before the Bible was written. Phillis's accomplishment as the first Black woman published in the American colonies is impressive, but it is also part of a long history of Black contributions to language and literature.

(One of these examiners was John Hancock, who later became the first person to sign the Declaration of Independence.) Only when they were convinced Phillis was intelligent and well-spoken enough to have produced her work did they lend their statement of support to her book.

Today, there are high schools, YWCA buildings, college dormitories, and literary clubs named for Phillis. (Just imagine what a star she would have been on social media today.) But people continue to give more credit to Phillis's supporters than to the writer herself. They say that, although she was enslaved, she was lucky to have had owners who recognized how bright she was. But Phillis would have been just as intelligent had she never been kidnapped. And she had to be a pretty incredible person and writer to impress kings, statesmen, and future presidents. Who knows what she might have accomplished if she had been allowed to live out her life in freedom.

The people who were lucky were the ones who met Phillis and got to enjoy her poetry.

She was one of the first women poets in this country, paving the way for women like Emily Dickinson and Louisa May Alcott. And every Black poet in the United States has followed in her footsteps. Phillis lived a tough life that was all too brief. But her powerful words still echo throughout history.

SOJOURNER TRUTH

ACTIVIST, PUBLIC SPEAKER, FAITH LEADER **BORN: 1797 · DIED: 1883**

- **Escaped slavery to become a world-renowned human rights crusader**
- **The first Black woman to successfully challenge a white man in court**

Knowing the right thing to do doesn't make doing it any easier. But for people like Sojourner Truth, the right thing is the only thing to do. When she escaped slavery, she weighed her obligations with her options. She fought in court for her family and her name, despite the system's being built for her opponent. And she worked tirelessly for the rights of others because she knew too well the weight of inequality herself.

Sojourner was born Isabella Baumfree to enslaved parents in Dutch-speaking Ulster County, New York. By the time she was 13 years old, she had been bought and sold four times. And although she worked very hard for no money, she was still treated cruelly and was beaten by some of the families who enslaved her. Isabella's final owner, John Dumont, forced her to marry an enslaved man he also owned. According to the law at that time, the five children they would have together also belonged to Dumont. But the law was beginning to change as New York moved toward emancipating enslaved people.

Dumont promised Isabella her freedom would come on Independence Day in 1826. When he went back on his word, Isabella had an agonizing choice to make. Legally, she still belonged to Dumont. But he made a promise, and she would hold him to it. She walked away from Dumont with only her infant daughter, as her four other children were lawfully bound to him.

Dumont found Isabella in the care of Isaac

The Narrative of Sojourner Truth

"TRUTH IS POWERFUL, AND IT PREVAILS."
—SOJOURNER TRUTH

UNEXPECTED

Audiences would marvel at Sojourner's speeches, and not just in admiration of her cause. She was six feet tall and spoke so articulately that some white listeners actually didn't believe she was the one speaking. Newspapers wrote that she was a life-size doll, operated by invisible strings, and that a white woman hidden backstage was talking into a speaker for her. They may have been in disbelief, but Sojourner's words clearly left an impression.

and Maria Van Wagenen, who bought her freedom from him for $20. And when Isabella discovered that Dumont had illegally sold her son, Peter, it was the Van Wagenens who helped her file a lawsuit to get him back. She won, becoming the first Black woman to successfully sue a white man.

It was also the Van Wagenens who led Isabella to Christianity. By the early 1830s, she was traveling New York state to attend large church meetings. She would stand up in the crowd and speak eloquently about her faith (a tradition called testifying). The more she spoke, the more people wanted to hear her speak. In 1843, Isabella said the spirit of God had inspired her to preach the gospel and speak out against inequality under the name Sojourner Truth.

While Sojourner was speaking at events, she met other famous abolitionists (people who were against enslavement). One was a journalist named William Lloyd Garrison. Another was Frederick Douglass, a formerly enslaved person who had escaped and who also was a great public speaker. And both were newspapermen who encouraged Sojourner to

tell her story. Having never learned to read or write, Sojourner simply spoke while a woman named Olive Gilbert wrote everything down. The result was a memoir called *The Narrative of Sojourner Truth*.

Sojourner continued addressing large crowds, giving her famous speech "Ain't I a Woman?" during an 1851 speaking tour. The speech was written up in multiple newspapers, making her a national sensation. And because Sojourner's message against slavery had expanded to include the fair treatment of women, it also caught the attention of women's rights activists Elizabeth Cady Stanton and Susan B. Anthony, who would aid Sojourner in her work.

When the Civil War started, Sojourner used her speeches to encourage men to fight on the side of the Union and against those who wanted to secede to keep people enslaved. She also helped Black soldiers get the things they needed. Her work earned her an invitation to meet with President Abraham Lincoln at the White House. While in Washington D.C., Sojourner began working with the National Freedmen's Relief Association, an organization that helped newly freed Black people get settled and improve their lives. She also worked to end streetcar segregation and to secure land for formerly enslaved people.

Sojourner Truth was no puppet. She used her mind, voice, and unfailing moral compass to

help others and to do what she knew to be right. In a time before television or the Internet, she spread her messages of humanity and equality around the country through sheer determination. In doing so, she became the first famous Black female public speaker in the United States.

GO WHERE YOU'RE NEEDED

Eventually, Sojourner moved to Battle Creek, Michigan, to be near her daughters. She continued to speak out against inequality, always focusing her energy on the fight she felt needed her the most. When she grew worried that Frederick Douglass was focused more on the rights of Black men than the rights of Black women, for example, she took up the cause of women's suffrage. Picking up the slack ensured that no one was left behind in the fight.

MADAM C. J. WALKER

ENTREPRENEUR AND PHILANTHROPIST BORN: 1867 • DIED: 1919

- **Created hair care products specifically designed for Black women**
- **America's first self-made female millionaire and a generous philanthropist**

We can't always avoid problems or hardship. But as Madam C. J. Walker proved, it's what you do when faced with hardship that matters. She could have given in to the feelings of worry and defeat. Instead, she turned her problems into a million-dollar business that helped women and girls all over the world.

Madam C. J. Walker was born Sarah Breedlove, the fifth child of Owen and Minerva Breedlove in Delta, Louisiana, and their first child born into freedom from enslavement. Southern enslaved Black people were freed just two years before she was born. Unfortunately, Sarah's parents didn't have long to enjoy their freedom—they passed away by the time she was just 7 years old.

Sarah went to live with her sister, spending the next few years picking cotton and doing housework to earn her keep. But she couldn't stand living with her abusive brother-in-law. To escape him, by the time she was 14 years old, she had married a man named Moses McWilliams. By age 18, she had given birth to their daughter, A'Lelia. And at age 20, she was a widow.

In 1887, Sarah moved to St. Louis, Missouri, to be with her brothers and took a job doing laundry. As a single mom without any formal schooling, she understood the importance of education. So she made sure her daughter went to the city's public schools during the day while she began taking classes herself at night. Sarah knew she was capable of doing far more than laundry.

"I GOT MY START BY GIVING MYSELF A START." —MADAM C. J. WALKER

The million-dollar idea that lifted up Sarah—and so many others with her—came from another personal struggle: hair loss. She had consulted her brothers, who worked as barbers. She had purchased products and whipped up home remedies. And in searching for a solution, she had found a job with Annie Turnbo Malone, a successful Black entrepreneur who made hair care products.

The work took her to Denver, Colorado, where she met her second husband, Charles J. Walker. It also inspired her to experiment with her own hair care formulas and methods. And it just so happened that her husband, who

worked in advertising, had some ideas about how to market her new scalp conditioning and healing treatment, including that she call herself "Madam C. J. Walker."

With Charles by her side, Sarah spent an exhausting year and a half traveling all over the South to sell and demonstrate her treatments. In 1908, she opened her own beauty school—Lelia College—in Pittsburgh, Pennsylvania. By 1910, she had established the Madam C. J. Walker Manufacturing Company in Indianapolis, Indiana. And in 1913, Sarah traveled to the Caribbean and Latin America to expand her business and to lift up more women.

Her own trained beauty consultants were selling her products door to door, newspapers were running her ads, and Sarah was making good money at the helm. She also made national headlines by donating $1,000 of that hard-earned money to the building fund for a Black YWCA in Indianapolis. It was just the first of her many large philanthropic contributions.

A LITTLE PERSPECTIVE

Saying that Sarah was the first Black female millionaire might not sound as impressive when you consider that the most successful entrepreneurs today are worth hundreds of billions of dollars. But the value of money has actually increased over time. A million dollars in Sarah's day is equal to almost $30 million in today's money. That means that donating $1,000 to the YWCA fund then would be the same as donating $30,000 today. When you put it into perspective, you see both how successful *and* how generous Sarah was.

HARLEM HOME BASE

While Sarah traveled, A'Lelia was overseeing the construction of their new townhouse in Harlem, New York. The area would become an important hub of Black culture in the coming years, an era dubbed the Harlem Renaissance. After Sarah's death, A'Lelia transformed the house into a salon, or a supportive gathering place for artists and activists, as well as an event space for meetings and parties. The townhouse brought both people and businesses to Harlem, helping the area grow.

In 1916, Sarah left the care of the factory in the hands of her female manager and moved to Harlem in New York City, to be with her daughter. There, she joined the board of the New York NAACP (National Association for the Advancement of Colored People), a group that fought for human rights. Sarah worked with activists to pass laws against lynching (the mob-led hanging of Black people), contributing $5,000 to the cause and joining a group of leaders on a visit to the White House.

Although she died just a few years later, Sarah had already changed millions of lives. Not only were her hair care treatments safer and more effective than what most Black women had used before, her sales system also provided Black women a better alternative to working as maids or doing laundry. A Walker agent could be her own boss, learn about business, and meet new people. The women felt good about themselves, and the money they earned helped them take care of their families. And all of this was possible because Sarah looked for solutions where others saw problems.

W. E. B. DU BOIS

SCHOLAR AND CIVIL RIGHTS ACTIVIST   BORN: 1868 • DIED: 1963

- **Transformed the way American society viewed the lives of its Black citizens**
- **Used data to solve social issues among the Black community**

When you hear the term "Renaissance man," you can think of a person who is not only talented in many areas but also tireless in their efforts to think, to create, and to make something better. This could be someone like Leonardo da Vinci, who was a Renaissance artist, inventor, and scientist whose works and ideas impact us even today—or someone many centuries later like W. E. B. Du Bois. This Renaissance man used his education, innovative thinking, and dedication to his goals to help shape our world.

William Edward Burghardt Du Bois was born in 1868 in Great Barrington, Massachusetts. His mother's family had a lot of land and his relatives were from many nations, but the town he grew up in was almost all white. W. E. B. became the top student in his class, and his local church helped raise money for him to go to college. He was a shining scholar who excelled, and his enthusiasm for learning languages like Greek and German opened doors for him.

When he was 24, W. E. B. moved to Berlin, Germany, to continue his graduate work. There, he had to complete all of his studies in German. Spending so much time in a place that had a different language and customs than the United States meant experiencing new attitudes and perspectives. He said of his time there, "I found myself on the outside of the American world, looking in. With me were white folk— students, acquaintances, teachers—who viewed

"BELIEVE IN LIFE! ALWAYS HUMAN BEINGS WILL LIVE AND PROGRESS TO GREATER, BROADER, AND FULLER LIFE." —W. E. B. DU BOIS

the scene with me. They did not always pause to regard me as a curiosity, or something sub-human." Feeling accepted outside of the United States helped empower him. When he returned home to attend Harvard University years later, he became its first Black American student to earn a Ph.D.

W. E. B. started teaching sociology at the University of Pennsylvania in 1896. Sociology is the study of people and how societies and groups function and work together. It might seem obvious to think about those ideas now, but before W. E. B. came onto the scene and shook things up, people didn't give sociology much thought. During his time as a professor, he wrote an important book called *The Philadelphia Negro*. The book explained Black life in the city and all the things that made it unique, as well as its challenges.

The research W. E. B. carried out for the book marked one of the first times anyone had gone door to door to collect sociological data, particularly from Black subjects. Using the data he collected, W. E. B. wrote about Black and Brown people as equals to white people. He showed white scholars that there was more to Black people than what old-fashioned ideas would have them believe. He highlighted the vibrant cultures and good values Black communities hold just like everyone else. During a time when many American scholars had racist ideas and considered Black people to be less than human, W. E. B. radically changed the conversation.

W. E. B. helped start the National Association for the Advancement of Colored People (NAACP) in 1909. The NAACP was, and still is, an influential human rights group that seeks justice and equality for Black people in America. W. E. B.'s work never stopped. He

HERE, THERE, EVERYWHERE

W. E. B. traveled the globe to learn about the challenges of Black and Brown people in other countries. He attended, organized, and eventually became co-chair of Pan-African Congresses around the world in the early 1900s. The congresses fought for peace, human rights, and opportunity where they were needed. W. E. B.'s intellectual curiosity took him just about everywhere, but some of the greatest challenges that he faced were right here at home.

A FAIR VIEW

W. E. B. created an exhibit for the 1900 Paris world's fair. The exhibit was about Black life in America, and W. E. B. and his team gathered 500 photographs and dozens of vivid infographics to portray Black individuals and families in different parts of the United States. His goal was to let visitors know that Black people were civilized and cared about education, and that their families were important. This was the first exhibit of its kind, and it was an example of how W. E. B. took an opportunity to challenge dated, racist ideas and make a difference with his research.

wrote many books, including *The Souls of Black Folk*, which talked about the Black struggle of "always looking at one's self through the eyes of others"—or feeling the weight of racist ideas against them. W. E. B. became an influential intellectual, and in the late 1940s, he helped to get the United Nations to listen to the problems of Blacks in the United States.

W. E. B. never stopped learning, and he was still studying up until his death when he was 95. The day after he died, 250,000 people were gathered in Washington, D.C., for the protest called the March on Washington. As the crowd assembled at the Lincoln Memorial from their cars, planes, trains, and buses, they were told, "The old man has died." Everyone knew that meant W. E. B. Du Bois. No one had fought for human rights longer than he had, and his leadership and influence are still powerful today.

BESSIE COLEMAN

AVIATOR BORN: 1892 · DIED: 1926

- **First Black American woman and first Native American woman to hold a pilot's license**

- **Championed and inspired generations of Black aviators**

Siblings love to tease each other. Sometimes this can lead to squabbles or hurt feelings. For Bessie Coleman, it only dared her to show everyone what she was made of.

Bessie Coleman grew up in Texas in a family of 12 children of mixed Native American and Black American ancestry. Her father, a farmer, left when she was young to live in Indian Territory in Oklahoma. He wanted to escape the racism of the American South and its Jim Crow laws that limited the ability of people of color to vote, get good jobs, receive fair pay, and more. Bessie and many of her siblings stayed in Texas. She attended a one-room schoolhouse and helped her mom clean houses and pick cotton to get by.

When Bessie was 23, she moved to Chicago to work as a manicurist. Around this time, many American servicemen, pilots included, came home with stories of bold and daring adventures abroad, including breathtaking flight missions. Their stories filled her with wonder.

One day her brother dropped by her salon in a particularly cheeky mood. He'd been stationed in France in the army during World War I and saw how liberated French women seemed to be. He said French women were better than Black American women because they were allowed to fly airplanes. Bessie had lived her whole life with the cards stacked against her and she was tired of being reminded of her limitations. "That's it!" she snapped at her brother, making a bold decision then and there. "You just called it for me."

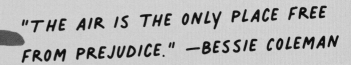

"THE AIR IS THE ONLY PLACE FREE FROM PREJUDICE." —BESSIE COLEMAN

OG FLYER

A lot of people don't realize Bessie Coleman got her pilot's license two years before a woman named Amelia Earhart, another bold early flyer.

After she was rejected by every American flight school she applied to, Bessie's resolve only grew. She would go to France. She'd have to take the flight test in French, so she started learning the language right away. She landed a higher-paying job as the manager of a restaurant and found financial support from local Black American business owners to pay for her aviation schooling.

After all her hard work and preparation, a school in Le Crotoy, France, accepted Bessie. She was the only person of color in her class, and, likely because of that, she was forced to learn in the oldest, most broken-down plane. Not one to be dissuaded, she learned how to do amazing tricks in the air, like loop-the-loops and tailspins. In 1921, at the age of 29, she earned her pilot's license and returned to the United States to much fanfare. The newspapers celebrated her as a "full-fledged aviatrix, the first of her race." But Bessie was just getting started.

Her dream was to open her own flight school. To raise money for the school, Bessie gave speeches about flying and showed films of her aerial tricks at theaters and churches. In 1922, she was the first Black woman in the United States to give a flight demonstration for a crowd. She flew figure eights and loop-the-loops to the amazement of adults and children alike. Some of the young spectators wanted to fly planes when they grew up. She did all she could to encourage Black Americans, in particular, to follow her path.

FRANCE

Name: Bessie Coleman
Date of Birth: 26th January 1892
Place of Birth: Atlanta, Texas

meets all requirements to hold an aviator's license.

"I MADE MY MIND UP TO TRY. I TRIED AND WAS SUCCESSFUL." —BESSIE COLEMAN

SETTING A HIGHER STANDARD

Bessie wasn't just a pilot; she was a voice for others. She did her best to represent and push for the rights of Black Americans, even when it made her job harder. If a theater or venue wouldn't seat Black people, she wouldn't speak there. When Bessie performed in her native Texas, the show promoters wanted to segregate the Black and white spectators in separate seating areas. Bessie refused to do the show unless the crowd was united. She met with the promoters until they changed their minds.

Bessie became so popular that she gave shows all over the country. At one of these shows in February 1923, her engine failed and her plane crashed. Bessie suffered some broken bones and facial cuts. When she healed, she went right back to touring again. Because of this, she was nicknamed "Brave Bessie" and "Queen Bess." In 1925, she had earned enough to purchase her own plane. By now, her brother probably had to eat his words.

On April 30, 1926, Bessie took a routine test flight with a mechanic named William Wills. When they were 3,000 feet up, a wrench got stuck in their engine. Mr. Wills was flying the plane and lost control. Sadly, Bessie fell out of the plane and died. Mr. Wills crashed and died nearby. When people heard the news, they heard more about the white mechanic who died than about Bessie.

Those who understood how incredible she was were very sad about the loss of the brave Black American aviator. A famous activist and publisher named Ida B. Wells spoke at

Bessie's large funeral service in Chicago. And in 1929, the Bessie Coleman Aero Club opened in Los Angeles. It was the first Black-owned flight school in the world. Bessie's dream had come true, but not in the way she expected.

Bessie Coleman blazed a trail that would inspire other women of color decades later. Mae Jemison, who became the first Black American woman to go to space in 1992, brought a photo of Bessie on the space flight with her. "I wished I had known her while I was growing up," Jemison said, "but then again I think she was there with me all the time."

LOUIS ARMSTRONG

- **Developed a way of playing jazz that influenced generations of musicians to come**

- **Brought jazz into the mainstream as a film star and comedian**

Not all trailblazers work in labs or on picket lines. Louis Armstrong, for example, changed the world through song. He was a musical genius on the cornet and trumpet. He came from humble beginnings to create his own brand of sound and to share his powerful, entertaining, and memorable voice with the world.

Louis Armstrong was born in New Orleans to Mary

Albert and William Armstrong. His dad left when he was just a baby. After spending his earliest years living with his grandmother, the junior Louis moved back to live with his mother, who was 21, very poor, and living in a neighborhood so tough it was called "The Battlefield." Later, when Louis was in the fifth grade, he dropped out of school and went to work to help his family pay the bills.

Louis found a job running errands

LAUGH WITH LOUIS

Louis liked to have fun when he sang. He'd impersonate street musicians, preachers, and riverboat comedians for his audience. He even made up little words to sing as he went along. He joked with the audiences and was popular with fans as a result.

for a local family named the Karnoffskys. He collected junk and delivered coal for them. They liked him so much that they treated him like a son. On his errands, he often heard music coming from the houses in the Karnoffskys' neighborhood. Some of it was a new music called jazz. Mr. Karnoffsky appreciated Louis's interest in music and gave him some money to buy a cornet, which is a type of horn.

Louis's life took a difficult turn when he got in trouble for firing his stepfather's gun into the air at a New Year's party. He was placed in a home for wayward boys. The boys didn't have mattresses to sleep on. The food there was horrible and the discipline was harsh. But one good thing did come from this experience: Louis received formal instruction on the cornet. Later, he said, "I do believe that my whole success goes back to that time I was arrested as a wayward boy. . . . Because then I had to quit running around and began to learn something."

When he was released from the home at age 13, Louis played his horn on the street for money and began to get noticed for his talent as a blues player. Joe "King" Oliver, a top-notch cornet player, was one of the most important people to see Louis's potential. He became a mentor for the young boy and did what he could to get Louis onstage. Soon Louis was playing at bars, parties, and dances. He had broken into the music scene at last. In the summer, he worked on a riverboat where a man named Fate Marable taught him how to read music. Shortly after, he started writing his own songs and singing them.

At age 21, Louis moved to Chicago to join King Oliver's Creole Jazz Band on second cornet. He soon made a name for himself in Chicago with his impressive sound and unique style. People noticed that Louis could blow higher notes than almost anyone. And he did it all while staying in tune. He could also hold the notes longer than most other players. In 1924, at the advice of his new wife, Lil, he left the band to join Fletcher

ONE OF A KIND

Louis had a voice no one could mistake for anyone else's. It was scratchy and strong. His unique singing voice and his lighthearted approach separated him from other musicians. This helped make him a star and encouraged other Black children to use their unique gifts as a door to opportunities.

Henderson's Orchestra, one of the most well-respected jazz bands in New York City. Louis took up the trumpet to blend in better with the others. He also tried the trombone.

In 1925, Louis and Lil moved back to Chicago, where he formed Louis Armstrong's Hot Five. Between 1925 and 1928, Louis made more than 60 records with his group. Today those records are considered a key chapter in the history of jazz.

Along with his thriving music career, Louis went on to perform in more than a dozen movies and regularly appeared on radio and television. His popularity proved that jazz could be a solo art. In 1971, Louis had a heart attack after performing in New York. Two months later, he died in his sleep.

Louis Armstrong's musical genius had a great influence on singers who followed in his footsteps, including stars like Bing Crosby, Billie Holiday, Frank Sinatra, and Ella Fitzgerald. He had an ear for rhythm, a talent for swing, and the ability to play high notes. He made scat singing (singing with made-up words) popular, paving the way for rap music to come. His songs, including "Hello Dolly" and "What a Wonderful World," are still part of our popular culture and appear in commercials and movies again and again. Louis's genius was as remarkable as it was timeless, and his music gave the world a new kind of rhythm to dream and dance to.

HE DID IT FIRST

Louis was the first Black American jazz musician to write an autobiography. It was called *Swing That Music*. He was also the first Black American to host a national radio show.

ELLA BAKER

HUMAN RIGHTS LEADER   BORN: 1903 • DIED: 1986

- **Helped unite and empower student activists with the formation of the Student Nonviolent Coordinating Committee (SNCC)**

- **Helped establish the Southern Christian Leadership Conference (SCLC) with Martin Luther King, Jr., and played a key role in the Civil Rights Movement**

We all notice things that are unfair about our world, but we don't always know how to fix them. Ella Baker had a special skill for teaching regular people how to change things for the better. Ella was an *activist*, someone who battles injustice or builds organizations that work to fix social problems. You may have heard of, or read about, the Civil Rights Movement of the 1960s, which was the foundation for the ongoing fight for racial justice that continues today. Ella developed not only one but two of the most important civil rights groups in the United States.

When Ella was a little girl, she lived on the land her grandparents had worked when they were enslaved. Her grandma, "Bet" Ross, told Ella stories of the hardships of those times. Grandma Ross had to do hard labor in the fields because she refused to marry the man her owner wanted her to. Bet and the man she chose to marry eventually purchased the land where they had been enslaved for $250.

Inspirational stories like these led Ella to value justice. She was inspired by her grandmother's courage in standing up for herself and learned to insist on being treated as an equal in a time when Black Americans were legally denied voting and educational

"GIVE LIGHT AND PEOPLE WILL FIND THE WAY." —ELLA BAKER

THE POWER OF YOUTH

Ella Baker recognized young people as a powerful force for change. She believed that young people were "the hope of any movement" and said they were the ones who "kept the spirit going."

rights. She also learned to listen to the stories of others and became devoted to their causes.

Ella was always a good student. Her mother, who was trained as a teacher, made sure of it. At the age of 15, Ella was enrolled in the high school program on the campus of Shaw University in Raleigh, North Carolina. She also went to college there, joining the debate team and writing articles for the campus newspaper. After graduating at the top of her class, she moved to New York City, where she became a social worker. This made Ella even more familiar with the problems faced by poor and Black citizens. She joined the Young Negroes Cooperative League, which helped Black people get the most out of their resources through cooperatively owned grocery stores, buying clubs, and other businesses. Ella believed that jobs and money were the best path to equality. "People cannot be free until there is enough work in this land to give everybody a job," she said.

Everywhere she went, Ella used her talent for planning and organizing. She started working at the National Association for the Advancement of Colored People (NAACP) as a field secretary. She was then promoted

to director of branches, becoming the most powerful woman in the organization. In that job, she got to know NAACP chapter leaders all over the country and formed a very important network of people who cared about civil rights. She also got to know ordinary people and made sure they were included and that their voices were heard. Ella believed in *grassroots organizing*, which means helping ordinary people band together to create political change.

In 1957, Ella moved to Atlanta to assist the famous civil rights leader Martin Luther King, Jr. She knew he had helped lead a protest against the bus system of Montgomery, Alabama, two years earlier after a teenage girl named Claudette Colvin and a woman named Rosa Parks had been denied seating

HISTORIC CONNECTION

Ella Baker and Rosa Parks both worked at the NAACP at the same time. The two strong women became friends. Ella mentored Rosa and encouraged her.

in the front of buses because they were Black. Ella suggested to Dr. King that he form an organization of his fellow ministers who opposed this kind of injustice. Because of her influence, the Southern Christian Leadership Conference (SCLC) was founded.

In 1960, four students from North Carolina A&T University in Greensboro, North Carolina, made international news. They demanded to be seated at a lunch counter at a Woolworth's store in downtown Greensboro that refused to serve Black people. Ella was inspired by their brave, nonviolent methods of protest and wanted to help encourage more students to do the same. She left the SCLC and moved back to her native North Carolina to help students get together and plan protests. Ella advised the leaders from the universities to start a group that later became the Student Nonviolent Coordinating Committee (SNCC).

Ella fought racial injustice and played a significant role in the Civil Rights Movement, but much of her worked happened

behind the scenes, not in front of cameras or microphones. She was not as famous as other civil rights activists, but that didn't matter to her. What mattered to her was progress. She listened carefully to the stories of Black Americans, learned about the struggles of ordinary people, and taught them how to fight their own battles. Ella often said, "Strong people don't need strong leaders."

As a leader, teacher, trainer, and advocate, Ella Baker changed the United States forever. She helped minorities organize to get better housing, higher-paying jobs, and fair voting laws. Through it all, she proved what an incredible impact an ordinary person can have.

A FITTING NICKNAME

Ella Baker's nickname was Fundi, a Swahili word for someone who passes down an important skill to the next generation.

CHARLES DREW

SURGEON AND MEDICAL RESEARCHER   BORN: 1904 • DIED: 1950

- **Improved techniques for both blood transfusions and blood storage**
- **Developed life-saving, large-scale blood banks during World War II**

Donating blood is a generous and noble thing to do. Your blood could help an injured or sick person come back from the brink of death. Fortunately, blood banks are now commonplace, and life-saving transfusions are available to many—all because of Dr. Charles Drew. By figuring out better ways to preserve the blood that people donate, Charles brought hope and progress to the medical field. Thanks to his research and innovation in the face of deep discrimination, countless patients have been saved.

Charles was the first child of a Washington, D.C., carpet layer named Richard Drew and a schoolteacher named Nora Burrell. His parents firmly believed in the value of a good education. Charles was a boy brimming with talent, especially in athletics. He won medals in swimming as a boy and he was an outstanding basketball and football player. In his high school yearbook, he was described as ambitious, popular, and athletic. By the time Charles was a junior, though, tragedy struck his family. His sister, who had been sick for some time with tuberculosis, died of pandemic influenza. Her death set the stage for Charles's growing interest in medicine.

Charles graduated from high school in 1922 and went to Amherst College in Massachusetts on a sports scholarship. He studied hard and was a star athlete in track and football, but he faced challenges that his classmates did not. He was one of 13 Black American students on a campus of 600 students. When he traveled to other schools for football games, some restaurants would refuse to serve him. The opposing teams would taunt him and take cheap

"YOU CAN DO ANYTHING YOU THINK YOU CAN." —CHARLES DREW

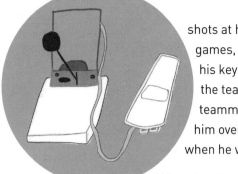

shots at him during games, and, despite his key role on the team, his own teammates passed him over as captain when he was a senior.

When Charles graduated from Amherst, he had learned valuable lessons about strength and resilience. He also knew that he wanted to become a doctor, which was no small feat or expense for a Black man at this time. He went to Baltimore to teach biology and to coach at Morgan College while he applied to medical schools. Eventually, his persistence paid off. McGill University, a top school in Montreal, Canada, accepted him and offered him a scholarship that made his medical studies financially possible.

Charles made good use of his time at McGill: he received two fellowships and was awarded his doctor of medicine and master of surgery degrees. His hospital research career began with an internship at Royal Victoria Hospital in Montreal, where he studied blood transfusions (the transfer of donated blood to a sick person) with another doctor named John Beattie.

Transfusions were crucial treatments for patients who had lost a lot of blood, needed major surgery, or couldn't make enough blood on their own. The problem doctors and scientists faced was that whole blood expired after just a few days. That meant that sometimes blood was wasted instead of being used to save lives.

Charles made it his goal to figure out a way to preserve blood for longer and to make transfusions available to more people. In 1938, he received a fellowship to study at Columbia University and to train at the Presbyterian Hospital in New York City. There, he studied human blood with other researchers and doctors. It eventually occurred to him that blood could be stored without its cells. Blood without cells (called plasma) could be preserved for about a week. Charles also figured out that if he dried the blood, he could store it and then return it to its normal form. Saving blood was called banking it (like banking money). He wrote a thesis called "Banked Blood: A Study in Blood Preservation." Other scientists called it a masterpiece. With his thesis completed, he was the first Black person to earn a medical doctorate from Columbia.

THE ROAD TO EXCELLENCE

Charles Drew knew that a Black man had to work harder than everyone else to prove himself, especially in medical school, where he was one of few people of color. So that's what he did. By the time he finished, he graduated from McGill University second in his class.

BIG BANKING

Charles was said to have collected roughly 14,500 pints of blood as part of the Blood for Britain program.

When World War II erupted, Charles was given the opportunity to put his research and findings to good use. He was asked by the Royal Air Force to set up a program called "Blood for Britain." He went to work collecting blood from New York hospitals, storing it in a way that prolonged its usefulness, and shipping it overseas to treat injured soldiers and civilians.

In 1941, the United States entered the war. The Red Cross asked Charles to make a blood bank, the first of its kind, to treat injured U.S. soldiers. Not long after he accepted this challenge, discrimination reared its ugly head. The military first refused to take blood donations from Black soldiers. Charles pushed back, but the military agreed to accept blood from Black soldiers only if it was segregated from white blood. Charles did not relent but stood by science and his morals. "There is no scientific basis," he explained, "for the separation of the bloods of different races except on the basis of the individual blood types or groups." He quit just a few months after starting.

Charles went on to create a surgery department at Howard University. While working there, Freedmen's Hospital (now called Howard University Hospital) named him its head of surgery. The NAACP (National Association for the Advancement of Colored People) gave him the Spingarn Medal to honor his incredible accomplishments.

In 1950, Charles died in a car accident on his way to a medical conference. He left behind a wife and four children as well as a legacy of life-saving innovation. Today there are schools, streets, college dorms, and awards named for him. He even appeared on a U.S. postage stamp in 1981. That's because Dr. Charles Drew is an American hero who helped save millions of lives with his discoveries in blood preservation. Just as importantly, he spoke up against injustice and never backed down despite the discrimination he faced along the road to success.

THURGOOD MARSHALL

U.S. SUPREME COURT JUSTICE   BORN: 1908 • DIED: 1993

- **First Black American member of the U.S. Supreme Court**
- **Successfully argued the case that ended racial segregation in schools**

As a young child, Thurgood Marshall learned a lot during family dinners. During the day, his father took him to hear court cases, where they sat in the gallery as spectators and listened to the lawyers' arguments. At dinner, the family would debate the issues. But Thurgood's father didn't just talk with his son. As Thurgood told it, "He turned me into [a lawyer]. He did it by teaching me to argue, by challenging my logic on every point, by making me prove every statement I made." It proved to be an important training ground for the bright young student.

As a top student at Lincoln University in Pennsylvania, Thurgood joined the debate team. As he had learned at his family's dinner table, he was convincing and made good arguments. Everyone could see he had the makings of a star lawyer. He also became active in civil rights issues, such as protesting against a movie theater in town that didn't allow Black customers.

Thurgood thought he could do his best work for Black citizens if he became a lawyer and worked to end discrimination through the court system. He wanted to go to the University of Maryland Law School, but it was only for white students. Instead, he went to Howard University Law School in Washington, D.C.

As a new lawyer, Thurgood worked for the NAACP (National Association for the Advancement of Colored People). The NAACP sued the University of Maryland Law School, the same school that wouldn't admit Thurgood

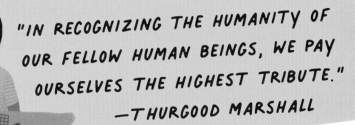

"IN RECOGNIZING THE HUMANITY OF OUR FELLOW HUMAN BEINGS, WE PAY OURSELVES THE HIGHEST TRIBUTE."
—THURGOOD MARSHALL

because he was Black, on behalf of another Black student, Donald Murray. Thurgood argued in court that the Blacks-only law schools were inferior to the University of Maryland Law School. He used the precedent set in an earlier case, *Plessy v. Ferguson*. In that case, the U.S. Supreme Court had ruled that facilities for Black and white people could be separate as long as they were equal in quality. (This became known as the "separate but equal" rule.) Thurgood told the judge in the law school case that either the Black law schools had to be equal to the quality of the white schools or the whites-only school had to admit Black students. He won the case, and Donald Murray was allowed to go to the University of Maryland.

Thurgood knew that not all Black people could afford to file lawsuits when they faced discrimination, so he started the NAACP's Legal Defense Fund. Now he could raise money to argue big cases that would affect the lives of many more Black citizens.

Thurgood won a lot of other civil rights cases before the Supreme Court, the highest court

in the United States, and he became one of the most famous Black lawyers in the country. However, in some towns, people threatened him. At night, cars driven by racist strangers followed him around. But Thurgood was as brave as he was bright—he continued to argue cases in Southern cities even when he knew his life was in danger.

Thurgood knew that a good education, like the one he got, was important for ending poverty and discrimination against Black people. So in the early 1950s, he asked people to write reports about, and send pictures of, the Blacks-only schools in their towns. Finally, in 1954, Thurgood got his chance to argue for

WHAT IS SEGREGATION?

After the Civil War ended and many enslaved people were freed, many states still wanted to keep Black people from gaining power. The Jim Crow laws made it legal to discriminate against Black Americans by denying them the right to vote, own houses, get high-paying jobs, or receive a good education. Black people couldn't occupy the same spaces as white people, a practice known as segregation. ("Segregate" means to separate or to keep apart.) Jim Crow laws were mostly in the South, but Northern states also discriminated against Black people. People who tried to defy the laws were often attacked, jailed, or killed.

A PRANKSTER

Thurgood loved to joke around. Twice he was suspended from school for pulling pranks on people. When he was on the Supreme Court, Justice Marshall used to greet Chief Justice Warren Burger every day by saying, "What's shakin', Chiefy baby?"

better schools for Black children in a landmark case called *Brown v. Board of Education*. He proved that Blacks-only schools were inferior to whites-only schools. Thurgood won again, and this time he changed the country. The Supreme Court said either *all* school buildings and classrooms had to be the same quality or Black and white kids had to be allowed to go to the same schools together.

Many governors in the Southern United States were against the ruling. Several ignored it. They didn't integrate their schools like the law said they had to. Where Black kids were allowed to attend white schools, some had to take school buses to neighborhoods that had been all white. And some faced violent mobs who didn't agree with the new law.

In 1967, President Lyndon Johnson nominated Thurgood Marshall to the Supreme Court. Most of the Southern senators didn't want Thurgood on the Supreme Court, but he finally won approval and became the first Black justice on the Court. He served for 24 years.

During that time, Thurgood helped change laws about the rights of people who are arrested. It is in part because of Justice Marshall that police have to read you your rights if they arrest you. Black law students and others looked up to Thurgood. People entered law school because they admired him. Today there are buildings, organizations, and even a law school named for him. And when Kamala Harris was sworn in as vice president of the United States in 2021, she took the oath of office on the Bible that once belonged to him.

Thurgood Marshall is remembered today as a brilliant judge and an important civil rights activist who helped end legal segregation in the South and made quality education available to Black students. So the next time your family is having a discussion around the dinner table, pay attention. It could change the direction of your life and you could end up changing the world.

"RACISM SEPARATES, BUT IT NEVER LIBERATES. HATRED GENERATES FEAR, AND FEAR, ONCE GIVEN A FOOTHOLD, BINDS, CONSUMES, AND IMPRISONS. NOTHING IS GAINED FROM PREJUDICE. NO ONE BENEFITS FROM RACISM." —THURGOOD MARSHALL

MAHALIA JACKSON

GOSPEL SINGER   BORN: 1911 • DIED: 1972

- Revered as the "Queen of Gospel" and one of the greatest musical figures in U.S. history
- Sang at the March on Washington at the request of Martin Luther King, Jr.

Mahalia Jackson was born in New Orleans, the granddaughter of enslaved people. She was raised by her aunt, who was a stern disciplinarian and very religious. They attended a strict Baptist church that did not allow jazz, card games, or drinking. Dancing was only allowed if a person was moved to do so by God. Mahalia joined the children's choir at age 4 and enjoyed the call-and-response music, which had a strong rhythm punctuated by clapping and foot-tapping. Mahalia said this music gave her "the bounce," which came to define her unique performance style.

Next door to her house was a very different musical experience. At the nearby small Pentecostal church, Mahalia could hear loud, exuberant singing, foot-stomping, and rhythmic hand claps. Instead of the organ, there were drums, cymbals, and tambourines. And instead of forbidding dancing, people sang with their whole bodies. Mahalia often stood outside to listen and said the music brought tears to her eyes. She also spent time at her grandfather's church, where the minister gave sermons in a "singing tone" that Mahalia said penetrated straight to her heart and strongly influenced her singing style.

When Mahalia was 10 years old, she dropped out of school to earn money for her family. She did laundry and scrubbed floors. But her life revolved around church and music, and she joined the church's junior choir at age 12. New Orleans was a very musical town. She heard

"WHEN YOU SING GOSPEL, YOU HAVE A FEELING THERE IS A CURE FOR WHAT'S WRONG." —MAHALIA JACKSON singers and blues and jazz pouring out of bars, people's homes, and during big street funerals, which were more like parades. Her older cousin collected records in secret, and when their strict aunt was out of the house, they played blues greats like Bessie Smith and Ma Rainey. Mahalia sang along and mimicked their style . . . until she found her own.

As a teenager, Mahalia moved with her family to Chicago. They joined another Baptist church, where people heard her powerful voice and expressive singing style. They asked her to join the choir. But soon Mahalia drew attention from the minister for her passionate singing style. The minister didn't like it, and told her she was "jazzing" up the songs. She also moved when she sang. Church members told her this wasn't appropriate and made her wear loose robes to hide her animated style. And when Mahalia finally saved enough money to hire a voice coach, he told her she was shouting and should sing songs so white people could understand them.

Despite the criticism, no one could stop Mahalia from singing the way she was meant to. She formed a quartet with three other church members, and they slowly built up a following performing at local churches and other events. She also found a mentor in Thomas Dorsey, a seasoned blues musician who took Mahalia under his wing. He trained Mahalia to sing more slowly for a greater emotional effect. They sang gospel music on street corners and tried to sell their music. Mahalia was also hired as a soloist for funerals and political rallies, including a rally for future president Franklin D. Roosevelt.

Despite offers for higher-paying singing work in other styles, Mahalia stayed true to her roots as a gospel singer. She turned down offers to sing in theaters (which she had been taught were "sinful") and with jazz bands such as Louis Armstrong's. And she refused recording offers to sing more popular music.

She continued to work with Thomas, and they toured the country performing concerts. In 1946, they did a show in Harlem, New York. A talent scout who was there got her a deal with Apollo Records. Back home, a big Chicago radio station started playing Mahalia's records and had her sing live. This helped introduce white listeners to her sound. Her record *Move on Up a Little*

UNFAIR TREATMENT

Life on the road wasn't easy for Black performers. Often in the South, Black musicians had to sleep in their cars because hotels wouldn't let them stay there, and Mahalia was no exception. She drove a Cadillac to make touring more comfortable. Because she drove a nice car, she was frequently stopped by the police and asked if the car was stolen. Banks in some towns wouldn't cash her checks because she was Black. Sometimes she had to carry thousands of dollars in her suitcases or under her clothes so she would have enough money to pay her living expenses while she was on tour.

WE ALL SING FOR ICE CREAM

Mahalia Jackson was upset when she learned that Black children in Virginia were unable to attend school because of violent conflicts over integrating Black and white schools. Even though she was home in Chicago, she arranged an ice cream party for children, singing to them over a telephone attached to a loudspeaker.

Higher became the second-bestselling record in the United States.

Mahalia continued recording music, which opened her up to even greater opportunities. President Harry S. Truman, who loved to play piano, invited her to the White House. A promoter asked Mahalia to sing at New York City's famous Carnegie Hall. No gospel artist had ever performed there. Her songs drew standing ovations and she set attendance records. Mahalia's music was played on Paris radio and she became an award-winning star in France, a first for a spiritual singer. Soon Mahalia was introducing gospel music to people all over the world.

Mahalia became active in the Civil Rights Movement and befriended Martin Luther King, Jr. She performed for free at events to raise money for Black organizations and appeared at important events, such as the Montgomery Bus Boycott, where Black residents were trying to integrate the city's buses in Montgomery, Alabama. And she was invited to sing "The Star-Spangled Banner" at John F. Kennedy's presidential inaugural ball in 1961.

On what would become a famous day in 1963, she sang at the Lincoln Memorial before Dr. King came out to speak. She was seated behind him on the stage, and said, "Tell them about the dream, Martin." Dr. King related his vision for the future of Black and white boys and girls in what became his legendary "I Have a Dream" speech.

Mahalia Jackson brought spirituals and gospel music to new listeners across the globe. She demanded fair treatment for Black citizens. Civil Rights and Black church leaders could count on her to draw and excite crowds and to raise money for worthy causes. The little girl who was told she was too loud had made her voice known around the world.

"WITHOUT A SONG, EACH DAY WOULD BE A CENTURY." —MAHALIA JACKSON

ELLA FITZGERALD

JAZZ SINGER   BORN: 1917 • DIED: 1996

- Known as the "First Lady of Song," she was the most popular female jazz singer in the United States

- Awarded the National Medal of Arts by President Ronald Reagan

Ella Fitzgerald seemed born for the stage. She loved to sing and dance and often went to see various acts at the Apollo Theater during their weekly "Amateur Night." In 1934, at age 17, she entered a lottery to appear onstage. She couldn't believe it when her name was picked. At first she thought she would dance, but after seeing the first act, the dancing Edwards Sisters, she changed her mind. She didn't think her dancing could compare. Her name was called and she walked out onstage, still not knowing what she would perform. She stood on the stage and stared at the audience, which began to shout and boo. Finally, she opened her mouth and began to sing "Judy." The audience quieted down and listened intently. They could hear the power in Ella's voice. When she was finished, the audience began shouting again, but this time they were yelling "Encore!" They wanted her to sing again.

The shy and quiet Ella had found the magic of performing. Offstage, she was self-conscious and insecure about her abilities. But when she got onstage, she

"JUST DON'T GIVE UP TRYING TO DO WHAT YOU REALLY WANT TO DO. WHERE THERE IS LOVE AND INSPIRATION, I DON'T THINK YOU CAN GO WRONG." —ELLA FITZGERALD

THE LEGACY OF THE APOLLO THEATER

The Apollo Theater is still an important cultural institution in Harlem. The Harlem neighborhood in New York City was home to many Black Americans who had left the South for a better life in cities in the North. The theater quickly became an important performance space for Black artists. In 1934, the theater started a weekly "Amateur Night," which soon became legendary. Many rising Black artists got their start at the Apollo, and Ella Fitzgerald was one of the first.

felt no fear. She was at home in the spotlight. And she knew performing was what she wanted to do for the rest of her life.

Ella's lucky break at the Apollo couldn't have come at a better time. When she was 15, her mother died in a car crash. She continued to live with her stepfather for a while but then moved in with an aunt. Shortly afterward, her stepfather died of a heart attack. Ella was very unhappy and began skipping school. She got into trouble with the police and was sent to reform school (an institution for young people as an alternative to jail). There she was beaten and mistreated. She managed to run away, but she was broke and alone, and the country was suffering through the Great Depression. Young Ella had to find a way to persevere, and music and singing became her ticket to a better life.

After her success at the Apollo, she was approached by the saxophonist from the band that night. He was impressed by Ella's talent and began

introducing her to people in the music industry who could help her career. Ella began entering—and winning—every singing contest she could find. The audience loved her. She was hired to tour and perform with a successful band. She recorded an album and performed at famous theaters around the country.

The popular jazz sounds of the time began to change from big-band performances to an emerging style called bebop. Ella played with this new style and began using her voice to imitate instruments in the band, especially the horns. She improvised onstage, using sounds and short nonsense words in her singing, a style known as scat. Her fans loved it, and this became her signature style. Her mastery of the style and a new album pushed her into the limelight, and she became famous in the United States. She hired a manager, and her fame began to spread around the world. She recorded albums with other famous jazz

Doo-ah doo-ah

musicians and brought her unique style to hit songs of the day.

As she continued to tour around the country, she was met with discrimination at hotels, concert halls, restaurants, and more. Police harassed her and her band because they were Black. They were even kicked off planes because of their skin color. Her manager refused to accept racial discrimination and insisted on fair and equal treatment for Ella and her band. Likewise, Ella fought to make sure that Black people could sit in the nightclubs and concert halls where she sang. In this way, she broke barriers for other Black musicians.

Ella continued to travel and tour all over the world. She recorded more than 200 albums and performed with many of the great musicians of her day. She got a star on the Hollywood Walk of Fame. In 1987, President Ronald Reagan awarded Ella the National Medal of Arts, the highest honor given to artists in the United States. It was one of her proudest moments.

Later, Ella reflected on her early challenges in life. She used those experiences to bring emotion and power to her singing. No one should have to go through the discrimination and roadblocks that Ella experienced in order to succeed. But Ella's voice echoes through airwaves and across generations to tell a story of a remarkable artist, one who sang her heart out and showed the world what she was made of.

A VOICE LIKE NO OTHER

In the 1970s and 1980s, a new generation of fans discovered Ella through her commercials for Memorex recording. In the ads, she sang notes so high they shattered a drinking glass. Then her voice was played back on the tape, and another glass broke. The announcer asked, "Is it live, or is it Memorex?" The ads showed people that the recording was so good that you could mistake it for a live singer.

KATHERINE JOHNSON

MATHEMATICIAN   BORN: 1918 · DIED: 2020

- **Calculated flight paths for some of the first manned missions to space**
- **Ensured the safe return of the first astronauts to land on the moon**

Some things in life can only be accomplished by a team: Winning a soccer match. Making a movie. Or sending a person to the moon. Sometimes, some people get more attention than others: the player who scores the winning goal, the star actors who draw fans, or the astronauts who land on the moon. But many team members work behind the scenes and that doesn't make their work any less important. Katherine Johnson was one such person. She worked quietly at NASA for more than 30 years, but her brilliant mind for math helped land the first spaceship on the moon—and get it back to Earth safely.

From the time she was young, Katherine showed a gift for math. Her parents and teachers noticed her talent, and they encouraged her to study hard. She skipped grades and entered high school at just 10 years old. By the time she was 18, she had graduated from college with a degree in math. She taught school, got married, and had children. Teaching might have been the extent of her math career if not for one fateful day in 1953.

When she was 34, Katherine heard that the National Advisory Committee for Aeronautics (which later became NASA) was looking for Black women to work on math problems. These math problems would be used to figure out how to get a spacecraft to orbit around the Earth and later fly to the moon. At that time, there were no computers like we have today. Math problems had to be solved by hand, using rulers and adding machines (which was

"GIRLS ARE CAPABLE OF DOING EVERYTHING MEN ARE CAPABLE OF DOING. SOMETIMES THEY HAVE MORE IMAGINATION THAN MEN." —KATHERINE JOHNSON

COUNTING HER WAY

As a child, Katherine first showed her love for math by counting. She counted everything: the number of steps it took to get to school, the number of steps into her church, even the number of silverware and plates as she washed the dishes. So much counting gave Katherine an ability to manipulate numbers in her head without writing them down.

all they had before calculators). NASA hired women because it could pay them less than men, and it hired Black Americans because it could pay them less than whites. These women were called "computers" because they computed the calculations.

In the 1950s, the United States and the Soviet Union (now known as the Russian Federation) were in a race to be the first to put a person in space and land on the moon. When John F. Kennedy became president, he announced that one of his goals was to land an astronaut on the moon before 1970. Kennedy said, "We choose to go to the moon . . . not because it is easy but because it is hard." Katherine was excited; she loved a challenge, and she knew her knowledge of math could help the NASA space program.

Katherine tried to learn as much as she could to help the space program. She asked to go to meetings where there had only been men. At first the men ignored her, until they realized how brilliant she was. As the first high-level Black mathematician

at NASA, Katherine was asked to work on the moon program. It was a top-secret assignment because the United States did not want the Soviet Union to know how close they were in the race to get to the moon.

One challenge of flying to the moon is that you can't fly in a straight line. Earth is spinning, and the force of gravity pulls objects toward it. The rocket needs to fly with enough power to escape Earth's gravity, then detach the capsule with the astronauts in it. Then the capsule has to circle Earth before continuing on a path to the moon. Afterward, the spaceship has to leave the moon and enter Earth's orbit before landing in one specific place on the entire planet. Katherine was working out how to accomplish these things on paper, mostly in her head. She was that smart.

The astronaut John Glenn was chosen to fly into Earth's orbit to make sure the spacecraft could make the trip. By this time, a gigantic computer had been invented and it came up with a route for Major Glenn's spacecraft to orbit Earth. Still, the astronaut told NASA to have Katherine check the computer's work. He thought her brain was even more powerful than a machine. He had that much faith in Katherine, and it was his life that was on the line.

On February 20, 1962, John Glenn safely circled our planet. Katherine's calculations had been correct. Major Glenn became a national hero and was invited to the White House to meet President Kennedy. Almost no one knew about Katherine and her role in the successful mission. Still, Katherine was part of a top-secret team, and she was not at NASA to become famous. She was proud, though. In 1969, she helped devise the path the *Apollo 11* astronauts used to become the first humans to land on the moon.

Katherine's own star finally began to shine in more recent years. In 2015, President Barack Obama awarded her the Presidential Medal of Freedom. She was nearly 100 years old. The United States had come a long way: from whites-only bathrooms to a Black president. In 2016, Langley Space Center named a building for her. A few months later, a book called *Hidden Figures* was published. It was about Katherine and the other Black women NASA used to call "colored computers." And in 2018, she was awarded a Presidential Honorary Doctorate of Humane Letters from West Virginia University.

Not long after *Hidden Figures* was published, it was adapted for the big screen and became an instant hit with critics and audiences alike. At the Academy Awards ceremony the next year, Katherine sat next to the actress who played her, Taraji P. Henson. When Katherine was introduced to the audience, they gave her a standing ovation. She had finally gotten the credit she deserved.

A LONG WALK TO THE BATHROOM

Katherine worked in a room with only Black women. The building where she worked, Langley Space Center in Virginia, didn't allow Black people to use the same bathrooms as white people. Katherine had to walk to another building for restroom breaks. This wasted a lot of her valuable time.

JAMES BALDWIN

WRITER AND HUMANITARIAN   BORN: 1924 • DIED: 1987

- **Brought much-needed attention to racial and social issues**
- **Used his writing to expose the truth of race relations in America**

James Baldwin was born in Harlem in 1924, the grandson of an enslaved person. He was the oldest of nine children in a poor family and had a troubled relationship with his strict, religious stepfather. To escape the family home, he spent much of his time in libraries and found a passion for reading and writing. As a teenager, he also became a preacher. Of those teen years, Baldwin recalled, "Those three years in the pulpit—I didn't realize it then—that is what turned me into a writer, really, dealing with all that anguish and that despair and that beauty."

Like other Black people during the first half of the 20th century, James endured many indignities of racism: poverty, violence, crime, despair, unhealthy living conditions, and few jobs or educational opportunities. Once he went into a restaurant where he knew they wouldn't serve Black customers. When the waitress refused to take his order, he threw a glass against the wall and walked out. He felt he could no longer live in the United States as a Black man and maintain his self-worth.

In 1948, at age 24, James moved to Paris, where he hoped he would be seen as more than just a Black man. In France, he felt he was treated more

"NOT EVERYTHING THAT IS FACED CAN BE CHANGED, BUT NOTHING CAN BE CHANGED UNTIL IT IS FACED." —JAMES BALDWIN

BLACK AND GAY

Another important part of James's legacy is his identity as a gay man during a time when homosexuality was still considered a "sin." He refused to be apologetic or ashamed. He said, "Everybody's journey is individual. If you fall in love with a boy, you fall in love with a boy. The fact that many Americans consider it a disease says more about them than it does about homosexuality."

like an equal. He also became friends with Europe's leading painters, writers, and filmmakers.

For the first time, he was able to get enough distance from his life in America to write about it. "Once you find yourself in another civilization," he said, "you're forced to examine your own." He finished his first novel, *Go Tell It on the Mountain*, about growing up in Harlem and the struggles of Black people. It was unlike anything that had been written before: he powerfully

described the humiliations, anger, and despair of Black Americans living in a racist society. Today, *Go Tell It on the Mountain* is considered an American classic.

While he was living abroad, James was closely following the news at home in America. The Civil Rights Movement was beginning, and James felt he owed it to his people to become an active participant in the struggle. He returned to the United States in 1957. He met and became friends with Martin Luther King, Jr., Malcolm X, and other important leaders of the Civil Rights Movement. He went to all the major civil rights marches and spoke out about racism.

In 1963, he published *The Fire Next Time*, a collection of essays. The title was named after a Bible prediction, and in the book James made a prediction of his own: he wrote that big cities in the United States could soon have angry riots. He knew that Black people felt unheard, and in their anger they would march through the streets and destroy property. James wrote, "The most dangerous creation of any society is the man who has nothing to lose." The book became a bestseller and was so electrifying that *Time* magazine put James on the cover.

James became an early and important voice in the Civil Rights Movement because he wasn't afraid to tell the truth about racism. He denounced violence and became a vocal advocate for equality. James was invited on TV shows to talk about how to solve racism. Viewers saw his quick mind and his skill with words. Anytime there was a major march, or a Black leader was killed, James was on TV speaking about it. When there were riots in cities like Los Angeles, Detroit, and Newark in the 1960s, some said James had predicted them.

James never stopped reflecting on, and writing about, racism in white America. He vividly described the pain and struggle of Black Americans in eloquent, passionate language. And his voice lives on in his numerous essays, novels, plays, poetry, and public speeches.

"YOU HAVE TO DECIDE WHO YOU ARE AND FORCE THE WORLD TO DEAL WITH YOU, NOT WITH ITS IDEA OF YOU." —JAMES BALDWIN

SHIRLEY CHISHOLM

CONGRESSWOMAN BORN: 1924 • DIED: 2005

- **First Black woman elected to the U.S. Congress, serving seven terms**
- **First Black person—male or female—to run for president of the United States**

Shirley Chisholm began her career as a teacher, where she learned about the needs of children, Black Americans, and poor families. Shirley used this knowledge and experience to improve her country. She went from being a great teacher to being an even greater leader.

Shirley was born in 1924 in Brooklyn, New York. Her father was from Guyana, a country in South America, and her mother was from Barbados, an island in the Caribbean. Her family was poor and her parents had trouble caring for their four children and working full time. So when Shirley was 5 years old, she and two of her younger sisters were sent to Barbados to live with their grandmother. It was an important experience in Shirley's young life. Years later, she said, "Granny gave me strength, dignity, and love. I learned from an early age that I was somebody. I didn't need the Black revolution to tell me that."

In Barbados, the teachers were strict and students were expected to do their absolute best. It prepared Shirley for the rest of her schooling, and she excelled in high school, college, and graduate school.

As a teacher, she saw how hard it was for working mothers to get childcare. She observed how struggling families didn't always have enough to eat. And she saw how Black children had fewer educational opportunities than white children. This

"IF THEY DON'T GIVE YOU A SEAT AT THE TABLE, BRING A FOLDING CHAIR." —SHIRLEY CHISHOLM

inspired her to find ways to improve people's lives.

Shirley first got involved in politics in 1953. There were no Black judges in the court system in her hometown of Brooklyn. She and many others felt it was time to have Black representation in the courts, and so she worked to get a Black man, Lewis Flagg, Jr., elected as Brooklyn's first Black judge.

Next, Shirley wanted to help Black women achieve representation in government. So in 1964, she ran for the New York state legislature and she won. She was only the second Black New York state lawmaker. She studied issues and how government worked. As a speaker, she was proud of her Caribbean accent and her clever expressions.

SHIRLEY CHISHOLM for PRESIDENT "—to represent all Americans"

Shirley knew she could help more people if she were in Congress. In 1968, she ran for a seat in the U.S. House of Representatives. The other candidates had more money and influence than she did, but she used her passion and smarts to persuade people to elect her. Shirley rode around her district in a sound truck, speaking directly to people over a loudspeaker. She would pull up outside housing projects and announce, "Ladies and gentlemen . . . this is fighting Shirley Chisholm coming through." She became known as "Fighting Shirley," and she became the first Black woman elected to Congress.

When she arrived in Washington, D.C., however, Shirley did not get a warm welcome. She refused to be quiet and listen, as she was expected to do. "I have no intention of just sitting quietly and observing," she said. "I intend to focus attention on the nation's problems."

And she did just that. While in Congress, Shirley helped pass more than 50 laws that improved the lives of millions of

MISTAKEN IDENTITY

Sometimes when Shirley was at social events for Congress, the wives of other lawmakers would think she was there to serve food or get coffee. Shirley had to tell them that she couldn't bring them coffee because she wasn't a waitress, she was a congresswoman.

people. She is especially known for helping improve children's education and nutrition. She also championed equality for all races and genders. She co-founded the National Women's Political Caucus and served on important committees in Congress.

In 1972, Shirley decided to run for president. She wasn't taken seriously by most reporters and many voters. Instead, as a Black woman, she was viewed as a symbolic political figure. Shirley wasn't able to raise a lot of money for her campaign. She couldn't afford expensive TV ads. She was blocked from being in the presidential debates. And she wasn't able to get her name on the ballot in most states. Some of the men in a group called the Congressional Black Caucus asked her not to run because they thought a Black man should run instead. Shirley's response was that she would be "unbought and unbossed."

Shirley didn't win the election, but she showed people women should be taken seriously in politics. She became the first Black major-party candidate to run for president and the first woman ever to run for the Democratic Party's presidential nomination. Shirley's legacy has not been forgotten. During her inauguration in 2021, Kamala Harris, the first Black woman to become vice president, wore a purple dress in honor of "Fighting Shirley."

COMPASSION AND COMMON GROUND

When Shirley was running for president, one of her opponents was former Alabama governor George Wallace. George was a forceful supporter of racial segregation (separating Black and white people). He once proclaimed, "Segregation today. Segregation tomorrow. Segregation forever." While he was campaigning in Maryland, someone shot and tried to kill him. Rather than hating him for his racist views, Shirley visited George in the hospital while he was recovering. Her compassion allowed her to find common ground that they could both agree on and later George supported some of her bills in Congress.

SIDNEY POITIER

ACTOR, DIRECTOR, PRODUCER BORN: 1927 • DIED: 2022

- **First Black male actor to win an Oscar for Best Actor**
- **Changed the way Black people were portrayed in movies**

Sidney Poitier was the youngest of seven children on his family's farm in the Bahamas, a group of islands in the Caribbean. The family moved to the capital, Nassau, when Sidney was 10. It was the first time he saw a car, or lived with electricity, refrigerators, and toilets. And it is where he first saw a movie, which made a lasting impression on him.

When Sidney was 16, he moved to New York City. He took a job as a dishwasher. A waiter helped teach him to read; they sat every night after work and read the newspaper together. When Sidney couldn't afford an apartment, he slept on rooftops. Next, Sidney lied about his age so he could join the army during World War II. He was put to work in a mental hospital, but he became upset about how the patients were treated.

He faked a mental illness to get discharged from the military and returned to being a dishwasher. Yet all of his jobs and the people he met along the way would help him as an actor.

One day, Sidney saw a newspaper ad for the American Negro Theater, an all-Black theater company. Sidney struggled with learning roles, and he wasn't a good enough singer for musicals. His strong Caribbean accent also limited the parts he was offered. Sidney

"I ALWAYS WANTED TO BE SOMEONE BETTER THE NEXT DAY THAN I WAS THE DAY BEFORE." —SIDNEY POITIER

worked on his speaking voice and acting skills, and when he was 22, he was offered a role in a movie called *No Way Out*. He played a doctor treating a racist white patient. Sidney remembered his experiences working in a hospital and this helped him understand his role better. He got noticed in Hollywood and was offered bigger and better roles.

His next big role was in *Blackboard Jungle*, a movie about a tough public high school. Even though he was 28 at the time, Sidney was a good enough actor to convincingly play a student. Three years later, Sidney co-starred in *The Defiant Ones*. In the film, two escaped prisoners, one Black and one white, are shackled together. The men hate and distrust each other, but they have to work together to stay alive. Sidney and his co-star were both nominated for an Academy Award for Best Actor, and this was the first time a Black man had been nominated.

Sidney also performed in the theater and appeared on Broadway. He played the male lead in the first production of Lorraine Hansberry's *A Raisin in the Sun.* The play showed details of Black life that overwhelmingly white theatergoing audiences had never seen. It was also the first Broadway play to draw a large Black audience. It was a groundbreaking play that the *New York Times* later said "changed American theater forever."

Sidney continued to star in movies and plays that dealt with the Black experience in America. In *Paris Blues*, he played an American musician living in Paris and the movie contrasted American racism at the time with Paris's acceptance

MARCHING FOR CIVIL RIGHTS

In 1963, Sidney joined a group of Black movie stars at the March on Washington to protest racial discrimination. Martin Luther King, Jr., spoke at the event, and they became friends. From then on, Sidney used his fame and wealth to help raise money for civil rights.

In 2002, Denzel Washington won an Oscar for Best Actor, becoming only the second Black male winner by that time. In his acceptance speech he said, "I'll always be chasing you, Sidney. I'll always be following in your footsteps. There's nothing I would rather do, sir."

of Black people. In *Lilies of the Field*, he played a handyman who helps a group of white nuns build a chapel. For that role he won an Oscar for Best Actor—the first Black man to do so.

The year 1967 was a big one for Sidney. He starred in three movies that dealt with issues of race relations and he was the highest-paid actor that year. The first of the three movies was *To Sir, with Love*, which explored social and racial issues in an inner-city school. Next was *Guess Who's Coming to Dinner*, which showed an interracial marriage at a time when it was illegal in many states for Black and white people to marry. In his last film of that year, *In the Heat of the Night*, Sidney's character

shocked filmgoers by slapping a white man. These roles, and many others, changed the way white and Black audiences saw Black actors on the screen.

Before Sidney came to Hollywood, audiences had never seen Black actors playing educated characters. Most Black male parts portrayed butlers, lazy Southerners, or waiters on trains. The actors usually made exaggerated faces or smiles and spoke in heavy slang. Sidney's performances showed Black characters with dignity and intelligence: he played a teacher, a doctor, a detective, and more. He gave Black viewers a sense of pride, which helped white people realize Black people could hold all types of jobs. Even his slight accent made his characters sound polished. Above all, Sidney played men who demanded to be treated fairly. "I [chose] to use my work as a reflection of my values," he said. In doing so, he changed America's values.

"I WAS THE ONLY BLACK PERSON ON THE SET. IT WAS UNUSUAL FOR ME TO BE IN A CIRCUMSTANCE IN WHICH EVERY MOVE I MADE WAS TANTAMOUNT TO A REPRESENTATION OF 18 MILLION PEOPLE." —SIDNEY POITIER

MARTIN LUTHER KING, JR.

HUMAN RIGHTS LEADER   BORN: 1929 • DIED: 1968

- **World-renowned spiritual leader of the Civil Rights Movement**
- **Awarded the Nobel Peace Prize—the youngest winner at the time**

Many products have a spokesperson, usually an actor or an athlete. Organizations and social movements usually pick someone to be their spokesperson, too. Dr. Martin Luther King, Jr., had a gift for public speaking and rousing people to action, and this made him the spokesperson for the Civil Rights Movement of the 1960s. But it wasn't his idea; others had to urge him to do it.

Martin's grandfather and father were both pastors and he learned from them. Even as a small boy, Martin had a great voice, and he often sang or recited Bible verses in church. Martin was also very compassionate. He hated seeing other people hurting each other or feeling bad. And he had a quick and intelligent mind. He could memorize long passages of the Bible and he read dictionaries and encyclopedias for fun.

Growing up in Atlanta, Georgia, Martin had to endure segregation and outspoken racism. But when he was 15, he traveled to Connecticut for a summer job. He was amazed by the change he saw in race relations in the North compared with the South. He wrote to his father, "The white people here are very nice. We go to any place we want to and sit anywhere we want to." He wrote his mother, "I never thought that a person of my race could eat anywhere but we ate in one of the finest restaurants in Hartford. And we went to the largest shows there."

"OUR LIVES BEGIN TO END ON THE DAY WE BECOME SILENT ABOUT THINGS THAT MATTER." —MARTIN LUTHER KING, JR.

STANDING UP AND WALKING OUT

Martin's parents taught him to stand up against racial injustice. When a shoe store clerk told Martin's father that he and his son would have to try on their shoes in the back of the store, his father walked out without buying anything.

After Martin graduated from college, he studied to become a minister. He married Coretta Scott and they settled in Alabama, where they had four children. Martin became the minister at a church in Montgomery.

In 1955, a woman named Rosa Parks refused to obey a law that demanded Black passengers on Montgomery city buses give up their seats in the front to white passengers. Black leaders decided it was time to fight the segregation law. They held rallies and asked Black people in Montgomery not to ride the buses. Instead, they organized carpools, took Black-owned taxis, or walked to work. The protest needed a spokesperson. Martin was asked because he was such an electrifying speaker. After much thought and prayer, he agreed. He later said, "I felt an inescapable urge to serve society. I felt a sense of responsibility, which I could not escape."

The protest, called the Montgomery Bus Boycott, went on for months and made national, then international, news. Martin spoke to reporters, stated the passengers' demands, and became the face of the movement. Finally, after a year of lost income on city buses, Montgomery changed its law. Martin and Rosa were seen as heroes.

Black leaders in other racially divided Southern cities asked Martin to come speak there. Martin became a frequent TV news and talk show guest, was photographed for magazine covers, and was even invited to India to learn about peaceful protest. He led marches all over the American South. When marchers were violently attacked by police or onlookers, he reminded everyone that they were not to be violent in return.

In 1963, Martin was the main speaker at a civil rights demonstration of 250,000 people in Washington, D.C. That day he delivered his "I Have a Dream" speech, which was shown on TV all over the country. He said the United States had not lived up to its promises in the Constitution and Bill of Rights that all people were created equal. A year later, Martin became the youngest person ever awarded the Nobel Peace Prize.

On April 3, 1968, Martin was in Memphis, Tennessee, for another protest. He spoke at a large church rally the evening before the planned march and told the audience, "I've been to the mountaintop. . . . I've seen the Promised Land. I may not get there with you. But I want you to know tonight that we, as a people, will get to the Promised Land." The church shook with applause. But many people later believed that his words contained a premonition, a prediction that he was in danger.

The next evening, Martin and other Black leaders were standing on their motel balcony waiting for their ride to dinner. There was a loud bang across the parking lot and Martin fell. He had been shot by James Earl Ray, an escaped prisoner. At the hospital, Martin was declared dead. He was 39, leaving behind his wife and four young children.

As the news spread on TV, angry, shocked people took to the streets and rioted; others mourned and prayed in their homes. Martin's funeral in Atlanta was attended by enormous crowds, both inside the church and outside, where people flooded the streets to pay their respects. His speeches were played during the service and people all over the world grieved the loss of a great leader. Fifteen years later, his birthday was named a national holiday. Every year on MLK Day, in mid-January, he is celebrated as one of the most important and inspiring leaders in America.

COMMITTED TO NONVIOLENCE

Martin was committed to nonviolent resistance in his quest for racial equality. Nonviolent resistance meant refusing to cooperate with systems that promoted injustice and oppression. This was demonstrated when Black people refused to ride city buses because they were segregated. Martin believed that nonviolence was a "courageous confrontation of evil by the power of love."

TONI MORRISON

AWARD-WINNING AUTHOR AND EDITOR BORN: 1931 • DIED: 2019

- **First Black female senior editor at major publisher Random House**
- **First Black woman to win the Nobel Prize in Literature**

Toni Morrison loved words from the time she was a young girl. Her parents cultivated a love for language and storytelling by sharing traditional Black folktales and songs. And she read a lot. Reading would become a lifelong passion and inspired her to write her own books.

After years of teaching English, Toni started working as an editor for L. W. Singer in New York City. Singer published schoolbooks for a company called Random House. Two years later, Random House promoted her to senior editor, making her their first Black woman in that position. Toni helped bring Black writers to Random House in the early 1970s, which was a period of growth in Black literature and arts. Toni published the works of Black activists Angela Davis and Huey Newton.

When heavyweight champion boxer Muhammad Ali wrote his life story, *The Greatest*, Toni Morrison was his editor.

Toni had also been writing her own short stories and poetry since she was in college. In one story, Toni wrote about a Black girl who wished to have blue eyes. She worked on the story on and off for years and turned it into a novel, *The Bluest Eye*. The book was published in 1970, when she was 39. The book didn't sell well at first. Then the City

> "IF THERE IS A BOOK THAT YOU WANT TO READ, BUT IT HASN'T BEEN WRITTEN YET, YOU MUST BE THE ONE TO WRITE IT." —TONI MORRISON

WRITING YOUR OWN STORY

When Toni was about 2 years old, her family's landlord set fire to their house, while they were home, because her parents couldn't pay the rent. Her parents responded by laughing at the landlord rather than falling into despair. Toni's parents' response showed her that you can tell your own story about an event in any way you want.

University of New York created a new Black studies department and put the book on its reading list. Soon other colleges did the same, sales increased, and she started to get noticed for her powerful writing on the Black experience in America. Toni said, "I wrote my first novel because I wanted to read it."

More books soon followed, and with them came praise, awards, and fame. Her second book, *Sula*, about a friendship between two Black women, was nominated for a National Book Award. Her third book, *Song of Solomon*, followed the life of a Black man as he uncovered his heritage. The Book of the Month Club added this book to one of its lists. No Black writer had had a book on the list since 1940 (*Native Son*, by Richard Wright). *Song of Solomon* became a bestselling book and won the National Book Critics Circle Award. At

last, Toni wasn't just publishing other Black writers' work. She had become a famous, respected author in her own right.

Toni continued to explore issues of race and identity in her books. Her book *Tar Baby* was about the relationship between a wealthy, beautiful Black fashion model and a poor, jobless Black man. In 1987, Toni published her most celebrated work, *Beloved*. It was inspired by a true story about a Black American slave and won the Pulitzer Prize for Fiction. A few years later, after publishing *Jazz*, Toni won the Nobel Prize in Literature, which awards an author for her entire body of work, not just a single book. She was the first Black woman from any country to win the prize.

The awards and honors kept coming. In 1996, the National Endowment for the Humanities awarded her the Jefferson Lecture, the U.S. government's highest honor for an artist. In 1998, *Beloved* was made into a movie starring talk show host Oprah Winfrey. Also that year, Toni

Toni inspired two generations of writers. Her works caused people to think about family and race differently. Today, Toni is one of only a few Black women whose books are taught nationwide in high school and college literature classes.

was featured on the cover of *Time* magazine, making her only the second female writer of fiction and second Black writer of fiction to appear on the cover. In 2006, the *New York Times* voted *Beloved* the best novel of the last 25 years. President Barack Obama awarded Toni the Presidential Medal of Freedom in 2012.

STORYTELLING IN OTHER FORMS

Toni didn't just tell stories in her novels; she also wrote works for singers and composers. Her short opera, *Margaret Garner*, was based on her main character in *Beloved*. She wrote a children's book called *Remember* (about the 50th anniversary of a Supreme Court decision that Black and white children should attend equal schools together). And she collaborated on a collection of children's books with her son Slade, who was a painter.

DICK GREGORY

HUMORIST AND ACTIVIST BORN: 1932 • DIED: 2017

- **First Black comedian to perform in top nightclubs and on television**

- **Spent most of his life fighting for human rights, working closely with Martin Luther King, Jr., and Malcolm X**

Dick Gregory was a jokester all his life, and he learned how to use it to his advantage. In elementary school he learned how to use humor to defend himself against childhood bullies. "They were going to laugh anyway, but if I made the jokes they'd laugh with me instead of at me," he wrote in his 1964 autobiography. "After a while, I could say anything I wanted. I got a reputation as a funny man. And then I started to turn the jokes on them."

Dick was drafted into the army in the middle of his college years. His commanding officer noticed how funny Dick was and encouraged him to enter talent shows, which were put on as entertainment for the troops. Dick loved making people laugh and he won several of the contests.

After the army, Dick decided to develop his talent for comedy. He moved to Chicago, Illinois, where he became part of a new generation of Black comedians. He drew on racial issues, current events, and politics for much of his material, and he was able to poke

"ONCE I REALIZED THE VALUE OF MAKING PEOPLE LAUGH, I GOT VERY GOOD AT IT. FAST." —DICK GREGORY

NOT WITHOUT CONTROVERSY

Dick's humor was difficult for conservative white people to take and his act was considered controversial in some areas, especially the American South. He often brought his act to colleges and universities, but the University of Tennessee banned him from campus, saying his humor was "an outrage and an insult." Students at the university sued the school and Dick was allowed to perform.

fun at segregation and other forms of discrimination. While he was making people laugh, he was also making them aware of the Black experience. He traveled to different cities doing stand-up comedy and became very popular.

News about his act spread, and Dick appeared on late-night talk shows. One of the most popular ones was *The Tonight Show*. Usually, guests performed their act and then sat down with the host, Jack Paar, to talk. However, Black guests on the show had not been asked to sit down for an interview after a performance. Dick refused to perform on the show. Jack Paar personally called Dick and said he would interview him after his act, just the way he interviewed his white guests. Dick

agreed. He was the first Black entertainer to break this cultural barrier.

Dick used his celebrity to help civil rights leaders and went to protest marches that were happening around the country. He was often arrested at these protests, and because he was famous, he drew attention to the cause. He became friends with Martin Luther King, Jr., and other civil rights leaders.

Dick didn't just protest in support of Black people. He demonstrated for women's rights, Native American causes, and environmental issues. He protested economic injustice, the Vietnam War, and apartheid (segregation of the races) in South Africa. He even went on several hunger strikes, in which he refused to eat as a form of protest against injustice.

A SHORT POLITICAL CAREER

In 1967, Dick ran for mayor of Chicago, but he lost. A year later, he unsuccessfully ran for president of the United States. He wasn't on the ballot but ran as a write-in candidate for the Freedom and Peace Party.

Dick had a gift for using humor to change people's hearts and minds. For example, he often told this funny story to get people to understand the indignity of segregation: "Last time I was down South I walked into this restaurant and this white waitress came up to me and said, 'We don't serve colored people here.' I said, 'That's all right. I don't eat colored people. Bring me a whole fried chicken.' Then these three white boys came up to me and said, 'Boy, anything you do to that chicken, we're gonna do to you.' So I put down my knife and fork, I picked up that chicken, and I kissed it. Then I said, 'Line up, boys!'"

Dick helped open doors for a generation of Black comedians. A successful stand-up comic looks at things differently than most people. They observe how people and governments behave. They see the irony in situations. Dick used that comedic talent to open people's eyes to injustice and discrimination. And he did it all while making them laugh.

"ONCE I ACCEPT INJUSTICE, I BECOME INJUSTICE." —DICK GREGORY

NINA SIMONE

MUSICIAN AND ACTIVIST BORN: 1933 · DIED: 2003

- **Called the "High Priestess of Soul" for her incredible musical talents**
- **Used her music and stardom to convey messages of Black empowerment**

Just because something is always done a certain way doesn't mean it should always stay that way. And just because there are roadblocks doesn't mean there aren't ways around them. Singer, pianist, and civil rights activist and icon Nina Simone knew this as someone who had to cope with racism, bipolar disorder, and domestic abuse. And she used her gifts to tell stories through bold music that made an impact not just on popular culture but also on how people thought about racial equality.

Nina Simone was born Eunice Kathleen Waymon in Tryon, North Carolina. The daughter of Methodist preachers who believed in hard work, Nina was raised to carry herself with pride and to do the right thing. It wasn't long before Nina was drawn to the church piano at the early age of 3. With the guidance of a classical piano teacher and a keen ear for music, Nina began to show dazzling talent on the keys—quickly finding a love for classical greats like Chopin, Beethoven, and Bach.

After Nina graduated as valedictorian from her high school, she spent a summer at New York City's Juilliard School of Music. She worked hard there to audition for the renowned Curtis Institute of Music in Philadelphia, Pennsylvania, where she

"I HAD SPENT MANY YEARS PURSUING EXCELLENCE, BECAUSE THAT IS WHAT CLASSICAL MUSIC IS ALL ABOUT. . . . NOW IT WAS DEDICATED TO FREEDOM, AND THAT WAS FAR MORE IMPORTANT." —NINA SIMONE

A POWERFUL VOICE

As she prepared for her first recital at the age of 12, Nina recalled seeing her parents being asked to sit in the back of the theater because the front rows were reserved for white people. This was typical of the racist norms of the time, but Nina would not stand for it. She insisted that if anyone wanted to see her play for the crowd, then her parents better be sitting right up front with her. And so it was. Even before she began her singing career, Nina's voice had power.

MIDTOWN BAR

First time in Atlantic City

NINA SIMONE

1719 PACIFIC AVE.

+

THE ONE AND ONLY

STAN (THE MAN) FACEY

hoped to become a trailblazing Black female classical pianist. She failed the audition, and she believed that she had been denied admission due to racial discrimination. Although she and her family had put all their hopes into Nina's attending Curtis, she was not dissuaded by being denied—she took private lessons from a Curtis instructor and found jobs to pay for them.

Nina's world changed one night when she was 21. She was hired for a piano gig at the Midtown Bar & Grill in Atlantic City, New Jersey. She had never been asked to sing before, but the owner required it. Her soulful, silky voice and incredible piano playing thrilled audiences and began attracting attention near and

far. She had a style all her own, combining jazz, blues, and classical music in a way that ignited any room in which she performed. It was then that she transformed from Eunice Waymon into "Nina Simone." While Nina's world may have changed with that one request to sing, little did she know that she would also change the world.

Over the next several years, Nina became noticed by the recording industry. In 1958, at age 25, she made a record of the song "I Loves You, Porgy" from the opera *Porgy and Bess*. The single sold well, and it led to her releasing her debut album the next year called *Little Girl Blue*. The song "My Baby Just Cares for Me" was later used in a popular Chanel No. 5 perfume commercial.

Later, when she changed record labels, she had more creative control over her music, and she began recording many more albums. Some musicians do better when they sing in a studio; Nina was unstoppable when she performed live. She had a deep, emotional voice that moved listeners, so she released many live records that captured her spellbinding performances. She was nicknamed the "High Priestess of Soul."

Nina's music was often about her Blackness and about social issues. She did not set out to be an activist, but her passion for equality soon began to show up in her songs, which resonated with people. When civil rights activist Medgar Evers was murdered in Mississippi and four little girls were killed by racist terrorists in a church bombing in Birmingham, Alabama, Nina was so disturbed, she recorded a powerful song, "Mississippi

Goddamn," in response. When Martin Luther King, Jr., was killed, she cut a tune called, "Why? (The King of Love Is Dead)." In 1970, Nina wrote a song called, "Young, Gifted and Black," about Black children being the hope for the future. The song caught on, and for some events and activists, Nina's song replaced "Lift Ev'ry Voice" as the Black National Anthem. People even sang it at parties and teachers taught it to schoolchildren.

Nina was a gifted pianist who started off thinking she would become a classical concert performer, but she turned into something much more. She threw her full spirit into every song. She was a symbol of racial pride, and she sang music that had power. Her voice is unmistakable, and it is still used in advertisements and in films to create heavy moods or to send political messages. Nina's story is an example of how we can speak up about the problems in the world.

TRUE TO HERSELF

Nina wore her hair the way it naturally grew at a time when it was rare for Black women to do so. She spoke her mind in interviews and hushed audiences if they spoke during her performances. And she didn't shy away from being honest or passionate about causes that were important to her, even if it meant not having her songs on the radio in parts of the country that disagreed with her.

QUINCY JONES

MUSICIAN AND PRODUCER BORN: 1933

- **One of the first Black Americans to hold a top executive position at a major record label**
- **Co-founded the Institute for Black American Music (IBAM)**

Elvis Presley, Michael Jackson, and Frank Sinatra were three of the biggest acts in music history. Will Smith is one of the most popular actors of his time. Imagine if you could have worked with one of them—or better yet, had a hand in their success. Quincy Jones worked with all four, and even though he wasn't always the one onstage or in front of the camera, his amazing talent defined some of the most important events in modern music, film, and television.

Quincy Delight Jones, Jr., was born in Chicago in 1933, and it wasn't long before he had a knack for music. At the age of 6, he would put his ear up to the wall and listen to his neighbor playing jazz piano. By the time he reached high school, Quincy was playing the trumpet for the school band, and at 14, he was playing in a National Reserve Band. Around this time, he met someone else who would also go on to greatness—16-year-old Ray Charles—and the two became trusted friends and collaborators.

In 1951, Quincy went to college in Seattle on a music scholarship. After a semester, he transferred to Berklee College of Music in Boston. He played in Boston clubs and was invited to tour with a bandleader named Lionel

"IMAGINE WHAT A HARMONIOUS WORLD IT COULD BE IF EVERY SINGLE PERSON, BOTH YOUNG AND OLD, SHARED A LITTLE OF WHAT HE IS GOOD AT DOING." —QUINCY JONES

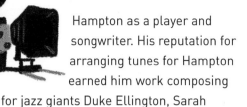

Hampton as a player and songwriter. His reputation for arranging tunes for Hampton earned him work composing for jazz giants Duke Ellington, Sarah Vaughan, Count Basie, and Dinah Washington. He was only in his early 20s, but he was already making waves; the new opportunities offered by playing with one big musician's band grew into a tsunami of a career.

At 23, Quincy took a job playing trumpet on a TV show with the Tommy Dorsey studio band. They played for Elvis Presley's first six TV appearances, which led to his number one hit, "Heartbreak Hotel." Quincy soon joined up with legendary trumpeter Dizzy Gillespie and his band, and they began a world tour sponsored by the United States government. When Quincy got back, he signed with a recording company and settled in Paris as a composer and music director. To some, playing in a big band all over Paris and the rest of Europe might be living the

dream. But with 18 band members, money was spread thin, so Quincy started to think bigger. He decided to focus more on producing music than playing it, and this move would change his career forever.

Quincy moved to Hollywood to concentrate on film work, writing the musical scores for many big films and television shows of the mid- to late-1960s. He also wrote jazz tunes, Latin music, and pop hits for teen icons. In 1978, Quincy created the music for a reboot of *The Wizard of Oz* called *The Wiz*. On that job, he met Michael Jackson, who was portraying the Scarecrow. The two soon teamed up to make Michael's album *Off the Wall*. Three years later, Quincy produced Michael Jackson's album *Thriller*, and it sold more than any album ever. Quincy also helped Steven Spielberg produce the movie *The Color Purple*, and he

VP STATUS

When Quincy took a job as a music director for Mercury Records, he may not have known that he was about to change history. In 1964, Mercury named Quincy as its vice president, making him the first Black American ever to be VP at a record company owned by white people. There is a reason why some people are called "trailblazers." Quincy did not have a path in front of him to reach this level, so he made one. And making a path meant he was making it possible for others to do the same.

is credited with bringing Oprah Winfrey and Whoopi Goldberg to the silver screen.

Quincy's star power meant he had connections. In 1985, he organized a fundraiser album called *We Are the World*. He got major stars of the time like Bruce Springsteen, Michael Jackson, Diana Ross, Bob Dylan, Tina Turner, Smokey Robinson, and Ray Charles to sing on the record. When all the pop legends crowded outside to enter the studio, Quincy made sure they knew he was boss. "Leave your egos at the door," he told them. This wasn't about the stars. It was about a good cause that they could all work

toward together. But the money from the explosively popular song didn't just help people in 1985. Since that year, "We Are the World" has raised over $63 million ($150 million in today's dollars) to help people in Ethiopia and other struggling countries in Africa.

Quincy went on to produce the sitcom *The Fresh Prince of Bel Air*. For decades, Quincy has produced concerts to raise money for charities, arts in the cities, and the Civil Rights Movement. In 2011, President Barack Obama awarded Quincy the National Medal of Arts. If you have heard ads, watched movies or cartoons, or seen YouTube videos, you have listened to the music of Quincy Jones. His work has touched people everywhere, and his trailblazing changed the world.

STOP THE MUSIC

No matter how hard you plan, you can't always see things coming. When Quincy was 41, he suffered a brain hemorrhage from an aneurysm. He had to have serious brain surgery. His family feared he would die, so they held a memorial service for him to celebrate his life. Not only did Quincy attend his own memorial but so did stars of the time like Marvin Gaye and Sidney Poitier. Six months later, Quincy had recovered, and he had a fresh sense of dedication to his work. Sometimes, tough experiences act as good reminders of what's important to us.

DIANE NASH

CIVIL RIGHTS ACTIVIST   BORN: 1938

- **Participated in, and organized, some of the most impactful moments of the Civil Rights Movement**
- **Winner of numerous prestigious awards for her activism, service, and leadership**

END SEGREGATION RULES IN SCHOOLS

Some people know their passions from an early age, like a fascination with computers or a love of the environment. But sometimes what a person is meant to do comes as a surprise, and it takes a series of events to bring out that passion. For Diane Nash, it was a change of setting that led her to become one of the most important figures in the Civil Rights Movement.

Diane Nash was born in Chicago in 1938. Growing up, Diane had a supportive family. Her grandmother instilled a strong sense of confidence in her and made her feel like the world was her oyster. Being a light-skinned girl from a middle-class family in Chicago, Diane hadn't faced as much discrimination as many other Black people of the time. It wasn't until she transferred to Fisk University in Nashville, Tennessee, as a college student that she began to see and feel first-hand how bad racism could be.

Diane started attending meetings near campus run by a minister named James Lawson. He taught Diane and other students about using nonviolent protests as a way to fight segregation laws. Nonviolent protest meant reacting peacefully to racists and rough police officers, even if they were violent toward the protesters. Diane became the leader of the

"THERE IS A SOURCE OF POWER IN EACH OF US THAT WE DON'T REALIZE UNTIL WE TAKE RESPONSIBILITY." —DIANE NASH

A WORLD DIVIDED

Segregation, or the separation of people based on the color of their skin, was the norm in the South in the 1950s. It was in Tennessee that Diane first saw lunch counters and department stores that would not serve Black customers. When Diane went to the Tennessee State Fair, the restrooms were separated for "white women" and "colored women."

"Every time I obeyed a segregation rule," Diane said, "I felt like I was somehow agreeing I was too inferior to go through the front door or to use the facility that the ordinary public would use." Diane looked for a way to change all this.

Student Central Committee of the Nashville movement. On other campuses, Black students were protesting in businesses that banned Black people. The protests were called sit-ins, and they made big news. In the spring of 1960, 22-year-old Diane led her own classmates downtown to sit in or march outside of stores and restaurants where only whites were welcome, bringing national attention to the Nashville movement.

Diane's voice mattered, and she didn't mince words. When she led a silent march of more than a thousand peaceful protesters in support of desegregation, she ended up face-to-face with the mayor of Nashville on the steps of City Hall. She asked him, "Mayor West, do you feel it is wrong to discriminate against a person solely on the basis of their race or color?" Her direct question surprised him and he told her he agreed that discrimination was wrong. The next day, newspapers echoed Diane and urged the mayor to stop segregation. A few weeks later, Black people were finally served at lunch counters around Nashville.

But the work wasn't done. Diane became a Freedom Rider—someone who fought for the desegregation of public buses in the South by riding the bus with other activists. In 1961, Freedom Riders in Birmingham, Alabama, were attacked by a violent mob, causing the peaceful protest to stop. Rather than be intimidated, Diane led the Nashville Student Movement Ride from Birmingham, Alabama, to Jackson, Mississippi. She said, "It was clear to me that if we allowed the Freedom Ride to stop at that point, just after so much violence had been inflicted, the message would have been sent that all you have to do to stop a nonviolent campaign is inflict massive violence."

Her Freedom Ride caught the attention of Martin Luther King, Jr., and she joined his group called the Southern Christian Leadership

Conference (SCLC). Through the hard work, sacrifice, and unwavering resolve of Freedom Riders and other activists, new laws went into effect on November 1, 1961, enforcing rules that allowed people to sit wherever they wanted on public buses. Diane continued to have an impact on the Civil Rights Movement alongside Dr. King and others. She played a role in the Selma Voting Rights Campaign, which influenced the Voting Rights Act of 1965 that enforced voting access for all people. President John F. Kennedy even appointed Diane to a national committee that led to the Civil Rights Act of 1965.

Diane eventually returned to Chicago, and it wasn't until decades later that her work was truly recognized. She has since received numerous awards for her impact on the Civil Rights Movement and her story has been featured in major movies. She continues to make a difference, advocating for fair housing and promoting nonviolence. Diane's driving force is an unwavering belief in nonviolence and sacrifice for others. She was a girl from a middle-class Chicago home, a former beauty pageant winner—a young woman who could have just avoided the struggle altogether. Instead, she became a force for good and helped change the course of history.

WE MARCH WITH SELMA

JAIL, NO BAIL

It was common for peaceful protesters to be unfairly arrested, which meant that Diane spent time in jail several times. In these situations, she had the option to sit in jail or to pay a fee ("bail") to be let go. Diane believed that paying bail supported the unjust system. Once, in 1961, Diane participated in a peaceful protest at a supermarket with other activists. Some white kids threw eggs at the activists. When the police came, they arrested 15 people but only five of the attackers. When the protesters were told they could be released for $5 bail, Diane refused to pay the bail and stayed in jail until they were all freed.

CLAUDETTE COLVIN

ANTI-SEGREGATION ACTIVIST   BORN: 1939

- **Refused to give up her seat on a segregated bus months before Rosa Parks**
- **Joined a lawsuit that helped end the practice of segregation on buses**

You don't have to be an adult to change the course of history. Sometimes, changing the world is taking a risk that others aren't willing to take, or just going with your gut when something feels wrong. That's what Claudette Colvin did.

Claudette grew up in Montgomery, Alabama. Just before she went to high school, her sister Delphine died of polio. Claudette was a good student, but her sadness from losing her sister made it hard for her to feel like a normal teenager and fit in. Claudette joined the NAACP Youth Council, where she started learning about the Civil Rights Movement. The NAACP (National Association for the Advancement of Colored People) was, and still is, an organization that worked on improving

Black people's lives and fighting for them in court. No one could have known what Claudette's quick thinking and tenacity would mean for the movement, but 15-year-old Claudette was ready.

Claudette caught city buses to school. Most of the passengers on these buses were Black, but if a white passenger got onto a Montgomery bus, Black riders had to make a seat available if all the others were taken. If that seat was in the front, the Black rider had to get off the bus and board again through the rear door. Sometimes the driver would take off while they were trying to do this. On March 2, 1955, on the way home from school,

> *"I KNEW THEN AND I KNOW NOW THAT, WHEN IT COMES TO JUSTICE, THERE IS NO EASY WAY TO GET IT." —CLAUDETTE COLVIN*

MIA IN ACTION

The MIA (Montgomery Improvement Association) was like a little NAACP for Montgomery. They helped Black people fight local wrongs. One member was a young preacher who had just moved there. He was 26, and his name was Martin Luther King, Jr.

Claudette got on the bus. After a few stops, a white woman got on and the whole bus was full. The driver ordered Claudette and three other Black women to the back. The three ladies moved, but a pregnant Black woman got on and sat next to Claudette. The driver got upset, insisting that they get up, and the pregnant woman refused.

When Claudette heard this, she also refused to stand. She later said, "It felt as if Harriet Tubman's hand was pushing me down on the one shoulder, and Sojourner Truth's hand was pushing me down on the other." Having just learned about courageous Black women who had also fought for justice, Claudette was filled with a sense of pride and conviction in that moment. The bus driver got

police involved, and when two officers came, Claudette still wouldn't budge. The police picked her up and carried her off the bus while she shouted, "It's my constitutional right to sit here as much as that lady. I paid my fare; it's my constitutional right!" Claudette would not be silenced.

The police handcuffed Claudette and brought her to the police station. On the ride there, they made nasty comments about her body even though she was just a child, and one officer sat in the back seat with her to intimidate her. She was charged with disturbing the peace, breaking the bus seating law, and battering and assaulting an officer. Claudette's classmate Annie Larkins testified in court that Claudette of course had not touched the officers. She was in fear during the ride that they would touch *her*.

A group of leaders met about Claudette's case. They got her a lawyer named Fred Gray, from the Montgomery Improvement Association (MIA). Still, Claudette was convicted on all three charges, although two of the convictions were later dropped. Claudette's pastor

told her, "Everyone prays for freedom. We've all been praying and praying. But you're different—you want your answer the next morning." It was Claudette's demand for justice that would bring it about.

In 1956, Claudette was part of a court case, *Browder v. Gayle*, that challenged Montgomery's transportation system as unconstitutional. Along with Aurelia Browder, Susie McDonald, and Mary Louise Smith, Claudette became a star witness in a case that went all the way to the Supreme Court. On December 20, 1956, the court ruling ended bus segregation in Alabama. Claudette was only 15 when she shouted that the treatment of Black people on buses was unconstitutional. A lot of people didn't want to listen to her because she was a kid, because she was Black, and because they thought she was a "troublemaker," but now the most powerful court in America agreed with her. Claudette eventually moved to New York, where she became a nurse and lived for decades as an unknown heroine.

Plenty of people stand up for their rights. Claudette Colvin sat down for hers. Her beliefs were based on the Constitution, her own sense of self-worth, and her knowledge of the brave Black changemakers who came before her. It took courage for her to do this. Without Claudette, leaders like Rosa Parks and Martin Luther King, Jr., may never have gained the traction they needed to build the Civil Rights Movement. Claudette changed the world because it was right, not because it was safe.

U.S. CONSTITUTION

It's my constitutional right to sit here as much as that lady. I paid my fare. It's my constitutional RIGHT!!

RING A BELL?

The details of this story might all sound familiar. That's because nine months later, on December 1, 1955, Rosa Parks was riding a Montgomery bus and did just what Claudette did—she refused to give up her seat. Dr. King used this as an opportunity to speak at churches and draw big-time attention to the racism of segregation, and so the Montgomery Bus Boycott began. Rosa Parks became the "First Lady of Civil Rights," and this was no accident. Having heard about Claudette's actions, the NAACP took an interest in this method of protest, but they decided that Rosa Parks—a mentor to Claudette—should be the face of the movement. She recalled, "They wanted someone . . . who would be impressive to white people and be a drawing [card] . . . like the main star. And they didn't think that a dark-skinned teenager, low income without a degree, could contribute."

MUHAMMAD ALI

BOXING CHAMPION AND SOCIAL ACTIVIST BORN: 1942 • DIED: 2016

- **Three-time world heavyweight boxing champion and Olympic gold medalist**
- **Awarded the Presidential Medal of Freedom for being a champion of both religious and civil rights**

Have you ever felt like you were born to do something great? Knowing is one thing. Identifying that unique purpose, planning to achieve it, and living it out even when the unexpected happens—that's a whole other fight. But it's one of many that Muhammad Ali won, thanks to skill, self-confidence, and dogged determination.

Born Cassius Marcellus Clay, Jr., in Louisville, Kentucky, he grew up believing he was meant to do something special with his life. Nothing about his surroundings indicated imminent fame or even success, though—he was a Black boy born to blue-collar parents in the segregated South. But a twist of fate and a lot of hard work helped

him become not just one of the greatest boxers of all time but also an inspiring social activist and humanitarian.

While 12-year-old Cassius and his friend filled up on treats at a local fair, someone else was making off with Cassius's brand-new bike. Infuriated, Cassius found a police officer and told him he'd like to catch whoever stole his new bike and "whup him good." The officer, Joe Martin, advised him that before he did

> "IMPOSSIBLE IS NOT A FACT. IT'S AN OPINION. IMPOSSIBLE IS NOT A DECLARATION. IT'S A DARE. IMPOSSIBLE IS POTENTIAL. IMPOSSIBLE IS TEMPORARY. IMPOSSIBLE IS NOTHING." —MUHAMMAD ALI

Cassius's well-known habit of hyping himself up before fights came from a true belief in his own abilities. As he put it, "It's not bragging if you can back it up." That confidence carried him through some even tougher battles ahead—like when he announced his relationship with the Black Muslim group Nation of Islam in 1964 (the same group to which human rights leader Malcolm X belonged). Soon after, he adopted his now-famous name, Muhammad Ali, which means *beloved of God*.

Muhammad saw the Nation of Islam as a celebration of Black heritage and a way to improve Black lives in a segregated society. He stood by his faith, even when it pitted him against the United States Department of Justice over his refusal to serve in the Vietnam War. "I will not disgrace my religion, my people, or myself," he explained, "by becoming a tool to enslave those who are fighting for their own justice, freedom, and equality."

any whupping, perhaps he'd better learn how to box. Luckily, Joe just happened to train young boxers at a local gym in his spare time.

With Joe's help, Cassius discovered that he was born to box. He went on to win the Golden Gloves tournament for novices, the National Golden Gloves Tournament of Champions, the Amateur Athletic Union's national title, and the light heavyweight Olympic gold medal—all before making boxing his full-time career.

PERSEVERANCE PAYS OFF

When Muhammad Ali was 16, he read in the newspaper that a noted trainer was coming to Louisville with one of his champions. Most teens would want an autograph. Muhammad wanted to learn. He called all the downtown hotels until he figured out where the trainer and boxer were staying, then he went to their hotel lobby and asked the desk clerk to call their room. Although perplexed, the trainer invited Muhammad up and answered questions about how many hours his fighters slept, what they ate, how many rounds a day they sparred, and how many miles they ran. Once Muhammad set a goal, he did whatever it took to achieve it.

BATTLING DYSLEXIA

As if going to school while becoming one of the best boxers of all time wasn't enough work, Muhammad also struggled with dyslexia. Later, in an effort to inspire kids like him, he and his wife, Lonnie, created a series of books and magazines written specifically to inspire young Black readers called *Go the Distance*. Muhammad believed that "Service to others is the rent you pay for your room here on Earth."

The boxing commissions stripped Muhammad of his title for evading service, and he could not fight for three and a half years—years he spent talking to people about his beliefs. As public opinion turned against the war, many started to see Muhammad differently, too. The sacrifices he made for his principles displayed courage and his journey changed how people thought about personal freedoms. In 1971, the U.S. Supreme Court ruled that denying Muhammad his religious freedom was unconstitutional. He called this his biggest victory.

Muhammad went on to win many more matches before officially retiring in 1981. Just three years later, though, he announced yet another real-life battle. He had been diagnosed with Parkinson's disease, a degenerative condition that sometimes caused him to tremble and his speech to slur. Despite obvious tremors, Muhammad still made history by lighting the Olympic flame with the ceremonial torch at the opening ceremonies of the 1992 Summer Olympics—to a standing ovation. He once again demonstrated to the world that, no matter the odds, you should never doubt Muhammad Ali.

Muhammad's contribution to history wasn't just his impressive 56 wins and 37 knockouts. It's also the way he never gave up. He fought for himself, for religious freedom, for Black Americans, for people in need, and for what he believed to be right. And he did it all while fighting personal battles. To Muhammad, nothing was impossible. He continued to advocate for change and to make the world a better place through charity work until his dying day.

"I AM THE GREATEST!"

ARETHA FRANKLIN

MUSICIAN AND ACTRESS BORN: 1942 • DIED: 2018

- Recognized as the "Queen of Soul," a genre that captivated the world in the '60s and '70s

- Recorded two songs that became anthems of civil rights and gender equality

The term "queen" usually applies to someone who was born into royalty. If it is about excellence in a skill, that person has typically mastered a talent for decades. Aretha Franklin was dubbed the "Queen of Soul" when she was just 22, and her reign has been recognized for more than 50 years.

Aretha Franklin grew up in Detroit, Michigan. Her father was a prominent minister named C. L. Franklin, and he was known widely as a powerful voice—so much so that he recorded sermons, drew the attention of activists, and became friends with Martin Luther King, Jr. When musicians were visiting Detroit, they often visited Aretha's father and performed casually in the Franklin living room. As a little girl, Aretha would sneak out of bed to hear stars like Dinah Washington, Count Basie, and Mahalia Jackson singing or playing in her home. In the early 1960s, Detroit was a beacon of Black music. Singers like Smokey Robinson and Diana Ross—who would become household names—were friends and

"BEING THE QUEEN IS NOT ALL ABOUT SINGING, AND BEING A DIVA IS NOT ALL ABOUT SINGING. IT HAS MUCH TO DO WITH YOUR SERVICE TO PEOPLE." —ARETHA FRANKLIN

A FRONT-ROW SEAT

Aretha had a front-row seat in the Civil Rights Movement. Her father, Reverend Franklin, worked closely with Martin Luther King, Jr., and in 1963 they led a huge civil rights march in downtown Detroit. Aretha participated, witnessing the first time Dr. King used the famous phrase "I have a dream," which would change the world at the March on Washington. Aretha and her family remained close to Dr. King, and she performed at his funeral in 1968. This firsthand experience would help define Aretha's stardom as symbolic for Black and women's equality.

lived right around the corner from Aretha.

It wasn't long before Aretha's musical talent started to shine. She learned to play the piano by ear when she was small, and she had musical greats surrounding her all the time. When she was just 11 years old, Aretha began touring as a soloist with her dad, and she released two recordings of gospel songs when she was 14. When Aretha was 18, she told her father she wanted to pursue a pop music career like Sam Cooke had. They both moved to New York City so she could try out for major record labels.

While Aretha's musical career was beginning to take off, she never forgot her background. In 1970, activist and public speaker Angela Davis was jailed, and Aretha offered to pay her bail for her release. Aretha said, "I have the money. I got it from

Black people—they made me financially able to have it— and I want to use it in ways to help our people." Her songs continued to top the pop and soul charts, and in 1972 she released *Amazing Grace*, which is still the bestselling gospel album ever. Aretha mastered jazz, spirituals, pop, and Latin music, and she was a gifted pianist and songwriter.

Aretha had some chart hits in the 1980s, after appearing in the movie *The Blues Brothers*.

When opera star Luciano Pavarotti was too ill to perform the song "Nessun Dorma" at the 1998 Grammy Awards, Aretha was asked to fill in for the Italian tenor. Despite such short notice, Aretha, a friend of Pavarotti's, sang flawlessly on the televised show and received a standing ovation. In 2009, Aretha sang "My Country 'Tis of Thee" at the inauguration of President Barack Obama. She made as many headlines for her fashionable hat as for her breathtaking singing. Ever the show woman, when Aretha sang "Natural Woman" at the annual Kennedy Center Honors in tribute to songwriter Carole King, she was so into the music that she let her fur coat fall to the stage floor during the performance.

Aretha Franklin's stardom belonged to everyone: the church community, soul fans, the women's movement, and the MTV generation. She was classically trained and operatically capable, but she was just as comfortable singing to tiny churches and blues clubs as she was singing to kings, queens, and heads of state. And all the while, she supported the hard work of social justice activists. When Aretha died in 2018, the major TV networks aired specials about her life and legacy. Stars from all genres of music honored her through emotional tributes. The Queen of Soul may be gone, but her music and legacy live on.

ARETHA'S ANTHEMS

Aretha catapulted to fame during two important movements: civil rights in the 1960s and the women's liberation movement of the 1970s. In 1967, Aretha released a cover of an Otis Redding song, but with her own touch. Aretha's "Respect" is considered one of the greatest songs of all time, and its lyrics spoke of equal rights in ways that made it an anthem of both gender and racial equality. Another song, "Natural Woman," would also become an anthem of the women's liberation movement. Aretha continued supporting Black causes, saying once, "Black people will be free. I've been locked up . . . and I know you got to disturb the peace when you can't get no peace."

STEVIE WONDER

MUSICIAN AND ACTIVIST   BORN: 1950

- **Transformed popular music with his innovative use of synthesizers and sound effects**

- **Used protest marches and testimony to help make Martin Luther King, Jr.'s birthday a federal holiday**

Sometimes, what someone else might call a weakness could actually be a person's biggest asset. Take Stevie Wonder, for example. Stevland Hardaway Judkins was born six weeks before he was due. He was put in an incubator until he could grow big enough to go home, but something went wrong. His retinas detached and he went blind soon after he was born. Rather than being held back by his lack of sight, Stevie let his hearing lead the way. Stevie would become one of the best musicians of his generation.

Stevie began singing in his mother's church at age 4, and he learned to play the harmonica, the organ, and the bongos, among other instruments. When he was 11, he sang a tune he had written, called "Lonely Boy," to Ronnie White, who was a member of a Motown group called The Miracles. White arranged an audition for the boy with Motown Records founder Berry Gordy, Jr. The record label signed Stevie and gave him the stage name "Little Stevie Wonder." The first album he released with some of his own singles was called *The Jazz Soul of Little Stevie*. Motown Records also worked with him on a tribute album to the famous blind musician Ray Charles. When the first album came out, Stevie enrolled in the Michigan School

"JUST BECAUSE A MAN LACKS THE USE OF HIS EYES DOESN'T MEAN HE LACKS VISION." —STEVIE WONDER

for the Blind, where he devoted himself to classical piano.

Stevie's music didn't sell well right away. When he was 12, he toured with older Motown acts on The Motortown Revue. The artists rode from city to city by bus. Little Stevie was a prankster, often sneaking up behind the adults and surprising them. In Chicago, Motown recorded a 20-minute

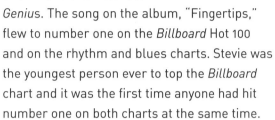

performance and released it in 1963 as part of the album *Recorded Live: The Twelve-Year-Old Genius*. The song on the album, "Fingertips," flew to number one on the *Billboard* Hot 100 and on the rhythm and blues charts. Stevie was the youngest person ever to top the *Billboard* chart and it was the first time anyone had hit number one on both charts at the same time.

After "Fingertips," Stevie's voice began changing and his record label considered dropping him. A songwriter named Sylvia Moy asked the head of Motown Records if she could write some music with, and for, Stevie instead. When he was 15, they released "Uptight, Everything's Alright," which rocketed Stevie Wonder back to the top of the charts. Stevie even began writing for adult Motown acts.

WONDER OF THE FUTURE

In the early 1970s, when Stevie was in his 20s, he began using technology to change the sound of his music. One of the machines he used was called a Computer Music Melodian, which was a synthesizer that mimicked instruments, sound effects, and the human voice. Other machines he used were the TONTO and Moog synthesizers. Stevie's synthesized tracks were an all-new way to make modern, funky rhythms and even made it easier for him to effectively be a "one-man" band. He also used unusual instruments, like the Hohner Clavinet, which is a keyboard that sounds like an electric guitar and is responsible for the unique sound in his song "Superstition." Stevie's sound was so transformational that its influence can be found across artists and genres, from Michael Jackson and Prince to today's pop and hip-hop stars.

> ## "YOU CAN'T BASE YOUR LIFE ON OTHER PEOPLE'S EXPECTATIONS." —STEVIE WONDER

Stevie's star status began to soar in the 1970s, and while he wrote many songs about love and family, he also became a master of social and cultural messaging in his music. His songs spoke about urban life in the United States, and he even sang about politics. In 1974, Stevie released a number one song called "You Haven't Done Nothin'." This song was a criticism of President Richard Nixon, who was later embroiled in a scandal and had to leave office. Stevie once said, "We all have ability; the difference is how we use it." He used his abilities to create trailblazing music that gave voice to people's concerns, hopes, and dreams.

After the death of Martin Luther King, Jr., Stevie recalled having a dream about making Dr. King's birthday a national holiday. Along with Dr. King's widow, Coretta Scott King, and other activists, Stevie worked tirelessly to make it happen. The activists spoke before Congress and organized marches every winter in Washington, D.C., to generate support for a nationwide observance of Dr. King's legacy. Stevie's 1980 single "Happy Birthday" was a huge success, but not because it was a catchy party song; it touched on Dr. King's good work

and why an official holiday was so important. Thanks in part to Stevie's efforts, Martin Luther King Jr. Day became a federal holiday in 1983 and was celebrated in all 50 states by 2000.

Through all Stevie's musical innovation, activism, and award-winning success, he never focused on his blindness. "I never thought of being blind as a disadvantage, and I never thought of being Black as a disadvantage," he said. "I am what I am. I love me!" He was the first artist to win the Best Album Grammy for three straight years, and he has collected many more. He has been inducted into multiple halls of fame, has sung songs that raised money for good causes, was recognized as the United Nations Messenger of Peace in 2009, and was awarded the Presidential Medal of Freedom in 2014. Throughout his life, he has kept up with changes in music, politics, fashion, and technology. That's how his songs stay current and his recording methods stay innovative. By using his art to get us to think about social issues and those less fortunate, Little Stevie Wonder grew up to have a wondrous impact on our world.

OPRAH WINFREY

INTERVIEWER, ACTRESS, HUMANITARIAN BORN: 1954

- **First Black woman to own her own production company and to make the Forbes list of billionaires**

- **Considered one of the most influential people of all time**

The beginning of a story is always important, but just because something starts off difficult doesn't mean it will always be that way. Oprah Winfrey can tell you all about that. Oprah was born in Kosciusko, Mississippi, to Vernita Lee, a housemaid, and Vernon Winfrey, who was in the military. Her given name was Orpah Gail, but people mispronounced "Orpah" so often that "Oprah" stuck. Changing her name wouldn't be the last time Oprah would make a meaningful transformation that would impact the rest of her life.

When Oprah was still a baby, her mother moved away to Wisconsin, and for several years Oprah lived with her grandmother. They were very poor, to the point that Oprah wore cotton sacks as dresses, and children often made fun of her. But her grandmother worked hard, teaching Oprah to read and write by the time she was 3 years old. At church, Oprah would recite passages from the Bible from memory and people called her "The Preacher."

Things continued to be hard for Oprah for a while. She moved back and forth between her parents' houses in Milwaukee, Wisconsin, and Nashville, Tennessee. She was abused by some members of her family, and

> **"CHALLENGES ARE GIFTS THAT FORCE US TO SEARCH FOR A NEW CENTER OF GRAVITY. DON'T FIGHT THEM. JUST FIND A NEW WAY TO STAND." —OPRAH WINFREY**

CURIOUS FROM THE START

Oprah is best known for her warm interview style that makes everyone around her feel comfortable. She has interviewed thousands of people from all walks of life—from celebrities and world leaders, to do-gooders and everyday folks, to refugees and people who are going through hard times. But she didn't just start off interviewing royalty like Prince Harry and Meghan Markle. Her ability to ask questions started with curiosity and a spark of imagination. As a little girl, Oprah would play with a doll made out of a corncob and ask it questions. She'd pretend to interview birds that were perched on her fence. You don't always know where imagination will take you, and for Oprah, it would take her to a career that would change the world.

CHICAGO

not everyone believed her. But by the time she reached high school, Oprah had returned to her father's house in Nashville and things started to take a turn for the better. She joined the high school speech team, she entered and won beauty contests, and a local radio station asked her to do news reports after class. She then won a speech contest that earned her a scholarship to Tennessee State University, where she studied communications.

When Oprah was 19 years old and still in college, she took a job as a newscaster, becoming the youngest person on the air in Nashville and the first female Black news anchor in the city's history. Over the next several years, she worked her way through

broadcasting jobs, and in 1983 she was asked to take over a daytime show called *AM Chicago.* In a few months, the show went from being the lowest-rated show at its hour to being the highest-rated show, unseating the long-standing ratings winner, a show called *Donahue.*

Soon, Oprah's talk show became *The Oprah Winfrey Show,* a national sensation that lasted for 25 years, from 1986 until 2011. Other shows of the time talked about national news, celebrities, or drama, but Oprah made her show personal. She spoke both to everyday people and to people who were changing the world, discussing anything from relationships and mental health to racism, women's rights, finance, and even cooking, health, books, and Christmas presents. She shined a light on what makes people more alike

OPRAH'S BOOK CLUB

HOW to Love the SKIN You're In

than different, and she listened to and encouraged anyone, no matter who they were.

It was said that everything she touched turned to gold, whether it was catapulting unknown authors' book sales with Oprah's Book Club, telling people her "favorite things" and making those products fly off the shelves, or giving a platform to other people who would become TV celebrities, such as Rachael Ray and Dr. Phil. Oprah founded her own production company, called HARPO (her name spelled backward), becoming the first Black woman ever to do so. She co-founded a women's television network called Oxygen, and in the early 2000s she started O, *The Oprah Magazine*, and her own network, called OWN, The Oprah Winfrey Network. Oprah has said, "Doing the best at

this moment puts you in the best place for the next moment." Her perseverance and hard work allowed her to make the most of her opportunities.

Oprah Winfrey is the most powerful woman ever in American media. She has produced movies, written books, and created products, networks, and charities that benefit people all over the world. In 2012, President Barack Obama awarded her the Presidential Medal of Freedom for her influence and devotion to giving back to others in need. Oprah had a rough start, but she did not let the sad parts of her youth hold her back. She used them to give her strength. Oprah's entertainment queendom proves that honesty and empathy are winners. Her hard work paid off, and she still makes sure to use her success to lift up others.

GUARDIAN ANGEL

Oprah's self-made success made her a billionaire, and she uses her position to help others. She started Oprah's Angel Network in 1998, which has since raised millions of dollars for hurricane relief, scholarships for the Boys & Girls Clubs of America, houses for Habitat for Humanity, school supplies and uniforms for impoverished children, and even book club books for kids all over the world. She started the Seven Fountains Primary School in KwaZulu-Natal, South Africa, which provides model education and state-of-the-art resources for more than 1,000 learners every year. When Oprah says, "Be thankful for what you have; you'll end up having more," she doesn't just mean you will have more for yourself—you will be able to create more for others.

FLORENCE GRIFFITH JOYNER

TRACK STAR BORN: 1959 • DIED: 1998

- Olympic gold medalist with world records in the 100-meter and 200-meter events

- Appointed co-chair of the President's Council on Physical Fitness

World records are made to be broken. When one person does something exceptional, they inspire others to follow in their footsteps. In the case of Florence Griffith Joyner—the fastest-running woman who has ever lived—women aren't just following in her footsteps, they're sprinting.

Florence Delorez Griffith was born in Los Angeles, California. Growing up in a big family with 10 siblings, she could have found it hard to stand out from the crowd. But Florence wasn't the type to blend in. From a young age, she had bold personal style. Her mother was a seamstress, and Florence loved fashion. When she was 7 years old, she began running track with the Sugar Ray Robinson Organization. She won the Jesse Owens National Youth Games not once but twice, when she was 14 and 15. As a teenager at Los Angeles's Jordan High School, Florence brought her flair for tights onto the track and encouraged her teammates to do the same. She began winning track meets, and her dedication carried over to college, when she commuted hours by bus to California State University at Northridge.

During her first year in college, Florence's track team won a national championship. Afterward, Florence had to make the difficult

"CONVENTIONAL IS NOT FOR ME. I LIKE THINGS THAT ARE UNIQUELY FLO. I LIKE BEING DIFFERENT." —FLORENCE GRIFFITH JOYNER

decision to leave college; she got a job as a bank teller to help support her family. But her coach, Bob Kersee, knew that Florence was destined for greatness in track and wanted to find another way. He was able to get financial aid money for Florence so she could attend the University of California at Los Angeles (UCLA) and continue to run track. With Kersee as her coach, Florence soon qualified for the U.S. Summer Olympic team in 1980 when she was 21 years old. So did her former Northridge teammates Alice Brown and Jeanette Bolden.

During the 1980 Summer Olympic team trials, Florence and her former teammates all qualified for the 100-meter event—with Alice in the lead and Florence finishing last. Florence missed out on qualifying for the 200-meter event by a slim margin, but it turned out that none of the women would go to the Olympics in the end. The United States opted out of the 1980 games in protest of host country Russia's politics at the time. Despite not attending the Olympic Games, Florence maintained her devotion to track. While she waited for the next Olympic trials, Florence finished her coursework at UCLA and graduated with a degree in psychology.

Florence prevailed in the 1984 Olympic Games held in Los Angeles, winning a silver medal for the 200-meter race. While she waited for the next Olympics, Florence returned to her work in banking and hairstyling. At the 1988 Olympic Games in Seoul, South Korea, Florence was the favorite to win the 200-meter and 100-meter races despite the fact that her friend, Evelyn Ashford, was ranked number one in the world.

FAST FASHION

Florence won races in a flash, but her flashy, unique style made her an icon for individuality and personal flair. Florence did not subscribe to the idea that a woman couldn't be stylish if she wanted to be taken seriously at her sport. She let her hair hang long, she adorned herself with jewelry, and she wore eye-catching, brightly colored bodysuits of her own design during her races. Her nails were nearly six inches long, with designs like tiger stripes, neon colors, and gemstones. Her energy and bright spirit showed as she smiled broadly during races. She had a style all her own and encouraged people to be themselves.

THE FASTEST WOMAN TO HAVE EVER LIVED

Florence carried the remarkable title of "fastest woman to have ever lived" for more than 30 years. In 1988, she set the world record for the 100-meter sprint at an astonishing 10.49 seconds. Florence also held the Olympic record for the same length, running the race in 10.62 seconds. But not everyone was excited about Florence's hard-earned success—some of her critics accused her of taking performance-enhancing substances to achieve her wins. Official tests and defense from Olympic doctors proved otherwise. At the 2020 Tokyo Games (held in 2021), Jamaican runner Elaine Thompson-Herah finally broke Florence's Olympic record by finishing the 100-meter race in 10.61 seconds. Florence's world title still holds, but a new generation of athletes is ready to accept her baton.

Florence was now married to triple-jumper Al Joyner, and announcers and fans had started calling her "Flo-Jo." Florence had refined her training and had become more muscular than in years past. She set a new world record in the 200-meter in the semifinals, and then broke it again in the finals, finishing in 21.34 seconds. In other words, she ran the length of two football fields in the blink of an eye. Florence won three gold medals and one silver medal at the 1988 Olympic Games.

Florence retired from track soon after the 1988 Olympic Games, when she was just 29, but she continued to leave a mark. In 1989, she designed the uniforms for the NBA's Indiana Pacers. She and her husband had a daughter named Mary. President Bill Clinton named her the co-chair of the President's Council on Physical Fitness, which encouraged kids to stay active. She started a charity called the Florence Griffith Joyner Youth Foundation in 1992 to support kids in need through track and field.

When Florence was 38, she died in her sleep from an epileptic seizure. The world mourned the loss of the fastest woman in the world and the style queen of track. Florence Griffith Joyner brought new fans to track and field. She was one of a kind, expressing herself and inspiring young girls while becoming a champion. Flo-Jo will be remembered for the spirit, style, and speed she brought to track, and for her inspiration to young athletes everywhere that you can be true to yourself while racing toward your dreams.

BARACK OBAMA

44TH U.S. PRESIDENT, NOBEL PEACE PRIZE WINNER   BORN: 1961

- **First Black president of the United States**
- **Lifted the United States out of one of the worst recessions in history**

CHANGE WE CAN BELIEVE IN

Some people are born to break boundaries, but they are not born knowing it. The first Black president of the United States of America wasn't born knowing what he would become. But a combination of family bonds, hard work, and unwavering ambition gave the world one of its most influential leaders.

Barack Hussein Obama was born in Honolulu, Hawaii, in 1961. His parents, Ann Dunham and Barack Obama, Sr., met as university students, but they were an unlikely couple for the time: Ann was a midwestern white woman and Barack Sr. was a Black man from Kenya. When Barack Jr. was just 3 years old, his father returned to Kenya and his mother eventually remarried an Indonesian man named Lolo Soetoro. They moved to Indonesia, where his mother tutored Barack with extra work and took him to all different types of religious services so he could learn about different cultures. Barack's life was full of learning from the start, and his mother was a role model he would always look up to.

Barack returned to Hawaii to live with his grandparents and his half sister, Maya. He called his grandma "Toot" and everyone called him "Barry." Barack worked hard in school and graduated from Columbia University in 1983. He moved to Chicago and became a community organizer, setting up job training programs,

"CHANGE WILL NOT COME IF WE WAIT FOR SOME OTHER PERSON OR SOME OTHER TIME. WE ARE THE ONES WE'VE BEEN WAITING FOR. WE ARE THE CHANGE THAT WE SEEK." —BARACK OBAMA

WHERE DO I BELONG?

The summer when Barack was 10 years old, his father visited him from Kenya for the first time since he was a toddler. But he didn't stay long, and Barack felt disappointed that they didn't bond. After all, Barack didn't look like anyone in his house, or like much of anyone in his school. He liked to watch the University of Hawaii's basketball team, which was mostly Black. Barack started playing basketball, and only when he was on the courts did he feel he belonged.

fighting for tenants' rights, and organizing tutoring for students who wanted to go to college. Barack went on to attend Harvard Law School, where he became the first Black president of the *Harvard Law Review*, a renowned law school publication. Around this time, he met his future wife, Michelle Robinson, and he stopped going by "Barry" and started going by "Barack." He was becoming more comfortable with himself and being biracial, and so was society.

Barack moved on to teach constitutional law at the University of Chicago Law School for more than 10 years. In 1995, he wrote a book called *Dreams from My Father*. In the book, he was honest about his struggle to fit in and about growing up with an absent dad. He began serving as an Illinois state senator, and in 2004, he was catapulted onto the national stage.

Barack served as a United States senator for the next four years, publishing a second book, *The Audacity of Hope*. In 2007, Barack ran a grassroots campaign for the presidency, and he harnessed the power of social media in a way that no candidate had ever done before.

He was driven by optimism, pledging plans for hope and change through hard work and unity. On November 4, 2008, Barack defeated Republican Senator John McCain to become the first Black president of the United States.

As president, Barack did things other presidents had not been able to do. He passed the Affordable Care Act, which gave millions of Americans access to health care. He ordered the search that led to the death of the terrorist Osama bin Laden. He pledged to slow climate change, he gave a path to citizenship to children of immigrants, and he won a Nobel Peace Prize. But there were also tough times. The economy was in bad shape when he entered office; banks closed and the automobile industry almost collapsed. The United States was involved in wars in Iraq and Afghanistan. Politicians and their voters were

WHO *IS* THAT GUY?

Barack gave the main speech at the 2004 Democratic National Convention. His words weren't just good, they were a declaration of hope for the future of America. During this speech, he said, "There is not a liberal America and a conservative America—there is the United States of America. There is not a Black America and a white America and Latino America and Asian America—there's the United States of America." Listening to him, people started to wonder if he could run for president.

very divided. It was hard to get laws passed because of all the disagreement.

Under Barack's leadership, the economy improved. Millions of people went back to work. Laws were passed that helped working women. President Obama also started the country back on good relations with nearby Cuba. When there were tragedies, such as natural disasters or mass shootings, the president traveled to where people were suffering and gave uplifting speeches. He was a family man who was sentimental about his mother and grandparents, loving toward his wife, and playful with his daughters,

Sasha and Malia. Since leaving office, Barack has written more books, started foundations, opened his presidential library, launched production companies and podcasts, and spoken all over the world.

Barack Obama gave hope to a country that was in need of it when he became president. His victory showed people that a child with an African dad and a white American mom, with a name that doesn't sound like "Bill" or "George," could be anything he wanted. The boy who felt so out of place got elected twice to a job you can't win unless millions think you fit in. And he opened a door to the future.

SURPRISE PARTY

When Barack won the presidency, the major television stations showed people in tears of joy. Many people said they never thought they'd live to see the day a Black person led America. Thousands of people gathered near the White House to be together. Unplanned celebrations broke out in 75 cities around the world. Indonesians, Kenyans, Hawaiians—and anyone else feeling the power of the new era of hope—were proud to have Barack Obama as the 44th president of the United States.

KAMALA HARRIS

- **First Black woman to be elected district attorney in California and first woman to be the state's attorney general, as well as the highest-ranking female U.S. public official ever**

- **First Black, Asian American, and female vice president of the United States**

A person who stands up for their beliefs is a strong person. A person who makes their beliefs their career is a force unlike any other. And Kamala Devi Harris is a force to be reckoned with. The sense of justice that would be her driving force throughout her life wasn't just something she learned growing up. It was in her blood.

Kamala was born in Oakland, California, but grew up just a few miles away in Berkeley—a town known for academics and activism. While she was growing up, her parents divorced and

her mother became the most important figure in Kamala's and her sister's lives, encouraging hard work, integrity, and connection to her Indian and Jamaican heritage. The mother and girls went to church as well as services at a Hindu temple. They traveled to Jamaica and to India. Kamala got to see how people lived in different parts of the world.

When Kamala started kindergarten, Berkeley began to bus some students to different schools to make the

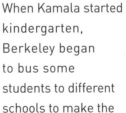

"ANYONE WHO CLAIMS TO BE A LEADER MUST SPEAK LIKE A LEADER. THAT MEANS SPEAKING WITH INTEGRITY AND TRUTH." —KAMALA HARRIS

A FAMILY OF FIGHTERS

Kamala's parents—Shyamala Gopalan, a breast cancer researcher from India, and Donald Harris, a college professor from Jamaica, met as doctoral students in Berkeley, California. When Kamala and her sister, Maya, were small, her parents would take them to demonstrations in support of the Civil Rights Movement. At one of these events, Kamala struggled in her stroller and began fussing. Her mother said, "Baby, what do you want?" Kamala shouted, "Fweedom!" This funny family story had flickers of what Kamala would become: a fighter for justice.

schools more diverse. Kamala took the bus to a town that was 95 percent white. Even though Kamala had her eyes wide open to different types of people, it didn't mean that everyone felt the same way about her. Kamala remembers that when she visited her father in Palo Alto, California, she was not able to play with neighborhood children because of her brown skin.

When Kamala was 12, her family moved to Montreal, where her mother taught at a college hospital and researched the genetics of breast cancer. Kamala went to a French-language school. There she witnessed how even more people lived. Kamala was a normal girl in a lot of ways; she was popular and she loved music, dancing, and cooking. She also worked hard and excelled. She went to the historically Black Howard University in Washington, D.C., in 1982, and then graduated from the University of California, Hastings College of Law.

As assistant district attorney in San Francisco, Kamala strived for fairness for all people. She didn't think kids should be tried in adult courts. Eventually, she would work in San Francisco City Hall, looking out for children who were in danger, and in 2002, she ran for attorney general of San Francisco against her former supervisor. Kamala said if she won, she would never give offenders a death sentence. She became the Golden Gate City's first Black district attorney.

And still Kamala strived for fairness. In 2010, she ran for attorney general of California and won. She was the first woman to win this office, and it was in this position that she set the tone for her support for the LGBTQ+ community. She fought against Proposition 8, which was a rule in California that prevented same-sex couples from marrying. Her efforts led the way to its removal, and as attorney general she was able to perform gay marriages. At the time, expression of support from a government official and political figure was still rare, but it mattered. In a few years, gay marriage became legal nationwide.

> "A PATRIOT IS NOT SOMEONE WHO CONDONES THE CONDUCT OF OUR COUNTRY WHATEVER IT DOES. IT IS SOMEONE WHO FIGHTS EVERY DAY FOR THE IDEALS OF THE COUNTRY, WHATEVER IT TAKES." —KAMALA HARRIS

Kamala won the U.S. Senate seat in California in 2017, and in 2019 she announced she was running for president. She appeared warm and upbeat at events, wearing a jacket, jeans, and Converse sneakers. She listened closely to people who spoke of their family or health struggles. She in turn spoke lovingly about her husband, Doug Emhoff, and her role as his children's "Momala." But Kamala couldn't raise enough money and left the presidential race at the end of 2019.

In August of 2020, Senator Joe Biden asked Kamala to be his running mate in the presidential election. The campaign quickly raised millions of dollars more in one day than Biden had during his whole campaign. The campaign was limited some by the COVID-19 pandemic, and there were feelings of division all throughout the country, but Kamala said, "Even in dark times, we not only dream, we do."

Kamala Harris has always aimed high and higher. Even when she found herself at heights no one her age, race, or gender had previously attained, she fought for her place and won. But one of her strongest guiding principles is to succeed with the intention of bringing others along with her. As her mother used to say, "You may be the first to do many things, but make sure you are not the last."

A MOMENT OF PRIDE

The Biden-Harris ticket won 81 million votes in the 2020 election, which was a record. In total, a record 150 million people voted during the COVID-19 pandemic, when many people had to vote by mail. On Inauguration Day, Kamala was sworn in as the first female, Black, and Asian American vice president. She became the highest-ranking woman in U.S. history, giving women and girls everywhere—and especially those with Jamaican and Indian heritage—someone to admire.

MISTY COPELAND

BALLERINA, AUTHOR, PHILANTHROPIST   BORN: 1982

- **First Black female principal dancer with the American Ballet Theatre (ABT)**
- **Pioneering voice for body positivity and inclusion and diversity in dance and athletics**

You never know what your story holds. For a 13-year-old girl living in a motel with her mother and five siblings, the idea of becoming a world-famous ballerina and an empowering role model would seem like a fairy tale. But for Misty Copeland, it would be a true story, and it was just around the corner.

Misty Danielle Copeland was born in Kansas City, Missouri, and was raised in San Pedro, California. In middle school, Misty became captain of her drill team and the coach noticed Misty's natural grace. She encouraged Misty to take the free ballet class at the local Boys & Girls Club. The ballet teacher, Cynthia Bradley, invited Misty to train at her small dance school, but Misty said no. With her mom working 14 hours a day without a car and her older sister juggling two jobs, there was no way for Misty to get to the studio. So Cynthia Bradley offered to pick her up from school to take her, and Misty's whole life changed.

Starting ballet at 13 years old is considered "late." But for Misty, her age didn't matter. It only took three months before she was dancing in toe shoes (*en pointe*). Developing her skills would swallow up time and money that her family didn't have, so Misty's mom told her she'd need to quit ballet. Luckily for Misty, the Bradley family invited her to stay with them on weekdays so she could continue practicing ballet, and on weekends she could take the

"START UNKNOWN, FINISH UNFORGETTABLE." —MISTY COPELAND

two-hour bus ride home to the motel in San Pedro to see her mom and siblings. This setup was huge for Misty's growth as a dancer, but it also came with a cost. Her mom and the Bradleys eventually got into a big battle over custody that landed them in newspapers and on television. But Misty persevered.

Imagine that you want to be an astronaut. You work as hard as you can, putting all of your dedication into reaching for the stars despite big odds, and suddenly NASA wants you to be on their team. This is what happened to Misty. She continued to work hard, competing in big-name competitions and attending intense dance workshops. Then, the American Ballet Theatre (ABT)—one of the best classical ballet companies in the world—offered Misty full scholarships to attend their summer programs while she finished school. She officially joined ABT Studio Company in 2001, where she performed in *The Sleeping Beauty*. Her hard work was paying off, but an injury would threaten to change it all.

Misty hurt her back and was forced to stop dancing for nearly a year. She was 19, and as with many athletes, the intense ballet training had delayed puberty (teenage changes in the body). During her recovery, she went through puberty and developed a curvy figure, and some ballet trainers said her body was all wrong for ballet. Misty suddenly felt ashamed. She got the sense that, as the only Black ballerina at ABT, with a different look from the white dancers, the trainers were also saying something about her race. Her confidence left her, and Misty became so self-conscious about her body that she struggled to dance. She even developed an eating disorder to try to look thinner.

When Misty started to feel better and love her natural body, the change was obvious in her performances. "I started dancing with confidence and joy. . . . And I think I changed everyone's mind about what a perfect dancer is supposed to look like." She was rising to greatness in part because how she felt on the inside showed on the outside. In 2007, when she was just

LOOK FOR THE HELPERS

Sometimes when you care about something, you don't always listen to the people outside of it because it feels like they wouldn't understand. But a new perspective can make all the difference. Misty needed help, and it was her friends outside of ballet who helped her heal her insecurities, take care of her body, and regain her confidence. Letting other people help you when you need it can make all the difference.

LIFE in MOTION: AN UNLIKELY BALLERINA
YOUR LIFE IN MOTION: JOURNAL
BLACK BALLERINAS
Firebird
LIFE IN MOTION
Bunheads   MISTY COPELAND

> "I WOULD WANT A YOUNGER CHILD LOOKING AT ME ON THE COVER TO SEE THEMSELVES. TO SEE ENDLESS OPPORTUNITY. TO SEE POSSIBILITIES THAT MAYBE THEY NEVER EVEN THOUGHT WERE SOMETHING THEY COULD ATTAIN. I WANT THEM TO SEE DREAMS THROUGH ME." —MISTY COPELAND

24, the American Ballet Theatre named her a solo dancer. Misty starred in big performances at New York City's Metropolitan Opera (known as "The Met"). She created her own roles in some ballets and she became the lead in others like *The Nutcracker* and *Swan Lake*—a ballerina's dream. She was even asked to dance alongside megastar Prince to the song "The Beautiful Ones" in 2011.

Because there were so few Black women in her art, Misty was rising to fame as a role model. She went on television and discussed her body image. Newspapers and magazines interviewed her. President Barack Obama appointed her to the President's Council on Fitness, Sports, and Nutrition to help kids stay fit and eat right. Women identified with her struggles with her body. Little Black girls looked up to her. Misty was showing the world something it had never seen.

In 2015, ABT named Misty its principal (star) ballerina—the first Black woman ever appointed—and she remains in that role to this day. This was a groundbreaking achievement, but Misty isn't finished making a difference. She has written several books, including *Life in Motion* and *Ballerina Body*, which describe her life as a dancer and how to have a healthy lifestyle. She has written children's books, too—*Firebird* and *Bunheads*, which tell stories of confidence through dance. She has worked as an ambassador for the Boys & Girls Clubs of America, and she continues to appear as an inspiring advocate for body positivity and diversity in different ways.

Misty Copeland overcame heavy odds—from starting ballet "late" and having family issues that made national news, to terrible injuries and body shaming, to being the only Black dancer in an art that was considered white. But when Misty was young, certain adults recognized her talent and supported her. Friendships made her feel better when she was having a hard time. And her dedication meant she never stopped trying.

ABOUT THE AUTHOR & ILLUSTRATOR

BIJAN BAYNE is an award-winning Washington, D.C.-based columnist and critic whose work has appeared in the *Washington Post* and the *New York Times*. He is the author of *Elgin Baylor*, the first biography of the basketball hero, which the *Christian Science Monitor* called a "book that inspires."

JOELLE AVELINO is a Congolese and Angolan illustrator and animator. Her animation project with Malala Fund was featured on *Design Weekly*'s list of favorite International Women's Day projects of 2020.